Painting
Garden Animals
in
Gouache

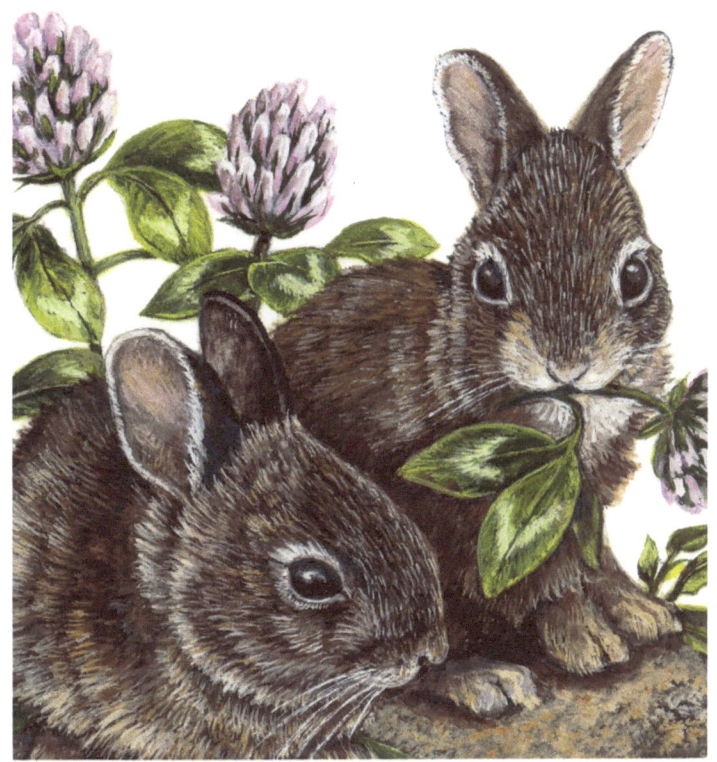

Written and Illustrated
by
Sandy Williams

© Sandra L. Williams 2015

Index
Garden Animals
in Gouache

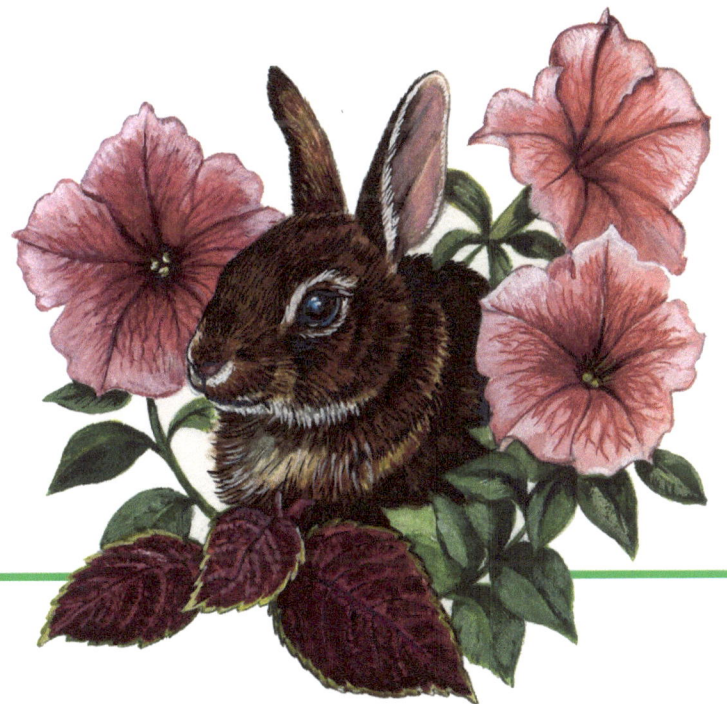

Introduction

Our gardens, small and large, make havens for many little wild creatures. They're part of the ecosystem we've created -- soil, flowers, bushes and trees that attract all sorts of insects, birds and animals. They create as much pleasure for us as the beautiful blossoms. In this workbook, I'll show you, step by step, how to create a detailed illustration of a White Footed Mouse, an Eastern Chipmunk and two young Eastern Cottontail Rabbits. I've included flowers in the illustrations but I've left them a bit stylized so you can concentrate on the animals.

This series of workbooks is meant to be a stepping stone. I can show you one way to do something but enjoy experimenting to see what works for you -- what most helps you create the piece of art you're aiming for!

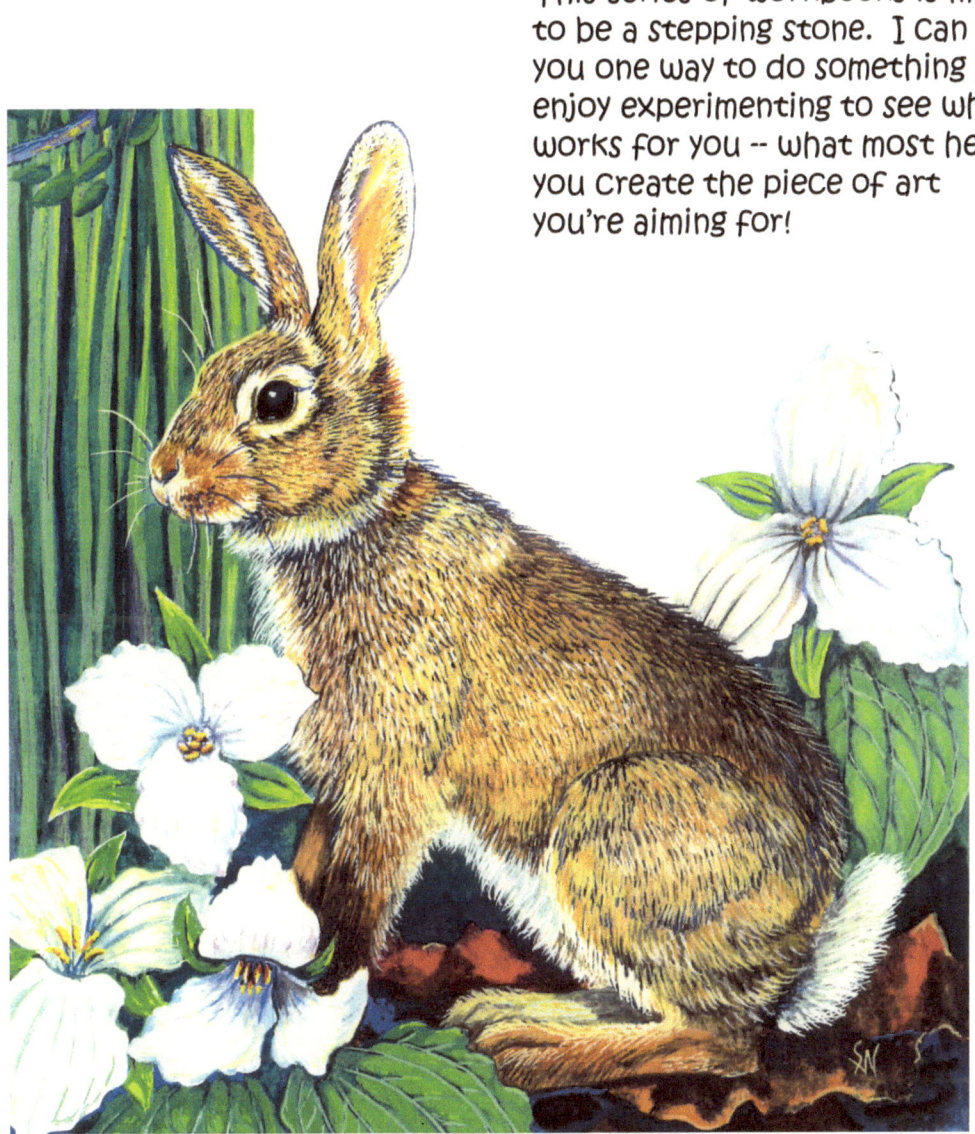

Gouache

(pronounced gwash)

I've tried many mediums to paint my detailed illustrations but I always come back to gouache, an opaque watercolor. Oils are beautiful and lush but painting in oils involves using chemicals that often have strong odors and the slow drying time can be a problem. Acrylics are fast drying but once dry they can't be reworked. Personally, I have a problem controlling transparent watercolor and it's very challenging for me. But gouache, with its colors that can be either brilliant or subtle, can be layered on and reworked even after its been dry for lengthy periods of time. Blending can make subtle variations in color and value and, along with precise detail, can bring your subject to life. Gouache is economical because, even after the dabs of paint have dried on your palette, they can be reconstituted with water so there's little waste. Because we often work with thick layers of gouache and sometimes use a "dry brush" technique gouache can be hard on brushes. Mine wear out quickly so I don't buy the most expensive ones -- just be sure you have the tiniest ones that can make a fine point. One of the great advantages of gouache is that it's very "forgiving." If you find that a certain area is not working just paint over it and start again.

Please note: It's easy to get lost in painting a detailed illustration, all bent over your work. But it's not good for the human body to sit in one place for long periods of time. Take frequent breaks -- get up and stretch, look at your work from a different angle. Also, don't forget, some of the pigments in many paints are toxic so don't point up your brush by putting the tip in your mouth.

Start by squeezing out spots of paint about this size

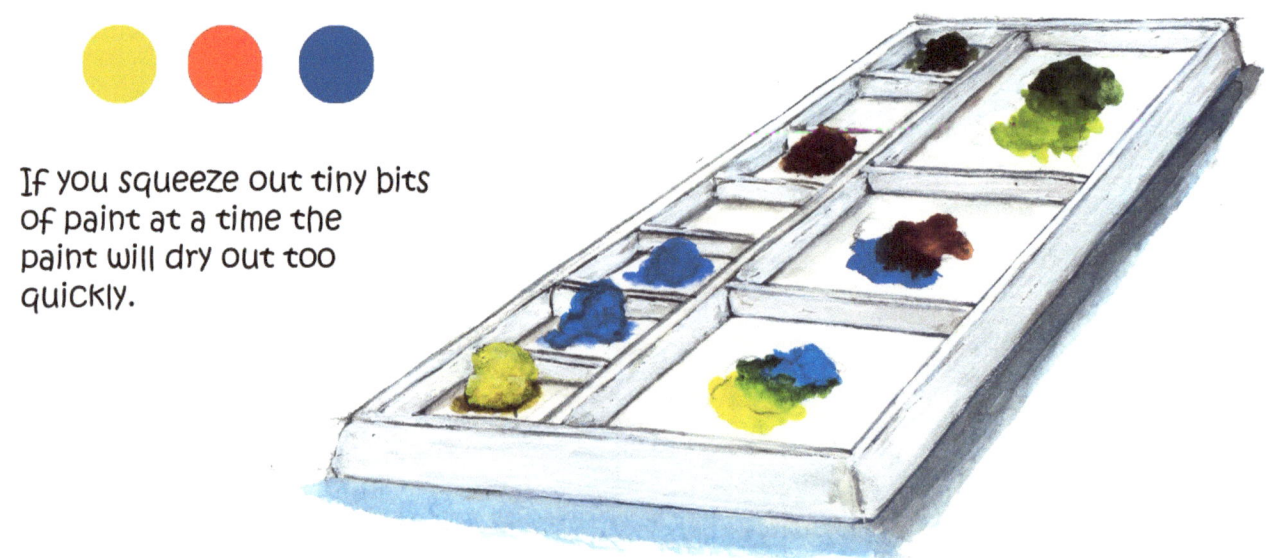

If you squeeze out tiny bits of paint at a time the paint will dry out too quickly.

Painting Garden Animals
Materials List

PENCILS -- I generally use a softer pencil, like a 4B, to draw with but use whatever you're comfortable with. Just make sure that you don't make your marks so hard that they're hard to erase. I use a kneaded eraser because it won't leave little crumbly bits of material that have to be brushed off.

PAPER -- I recommend using hot press watercolor paper, preferably 140 #, although a little lighter weight would be OK, too. Some artists use illustration board, vellum or bristol.   I use Arches 140# hot press because it has a nice, smooth surface to make detailing easier and crisper looking. Experiment and try some different papers. One half standard size sheet should be plenty for this course.

PALETTE -- It should be white so you can see exactly what color you're mixing. If you don't have a palette a white paper plate works fine. It's just a little harder to transport wet paint if you have to move around.

WATER CONTAINER -- Use whatever you have on hand. At home I use thoroughly cleaned plastic cat food containers-- no breakage problem.

TRANSFER PAPER -- Depending on how you transfer your images you may or may not need some plain tracing paper. An 11" x 14" sheet folded in half should do. Cover one side completely with soft graphite.

BRUSHES -- You'll probably need three small watercolor brushes: a 4/0 small round, a #1 small round and, if you can find one, a 20/0 round.

GOUACHE -- The nine tubes listed here will give you enough variety of colors to complete all the illustrations in this course. The brand I use is Winsor & Newton but that's not a requirement.

Permanent White	Opera Rose
Olive Green	Brilliant Violet
Burnt Umber	Ultramarine Blue
Burnt Sienna	Marigold Yellow
Yellow Ochre	

Color

Don't worry if your colors don't match those in this demonstration exactly. Color is ever changing -- the color of a chipmunk may be almost red if he's sitting in the sun but more of a dull brown if he's hiding in the shadows. One thing to avoid is a flat area of an even tone of color. This will look unnatural. These demonstrations will show you how to work in layers and blend them to make beautiful and subtle variations in color to make your subject look more realistic.

Value

Value is the lightness or darkness of the color you're working with. If your painting has almost all the same values it will lose contrast and may be dull or uninteresting. Be sure to use a full range in your work. You won't be using black in these demonstrations but will instead be using a mixture of Burnt Umber and Ultramarine Blue for the darkest values. To lighten this mixture you'll add White. See the illustration below to see the full range of values you can make using this important mixture.

Burnt Umber/Ultramarine Blue: light to dark

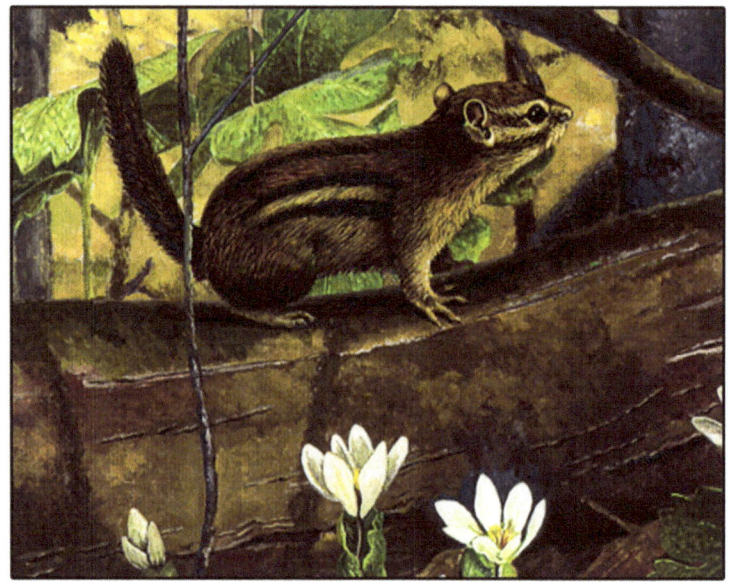

Underpainting & Blending

There are two very important techniques to learn when using gouache.

Underpainting -- For most of my illustrations I paint "light over dark." That means that, even though my subject may end up being white or a very light color, I still first paint it with a dark value gouache, usually a mixture of Burnt Umber and Ultramarine Blue. If I'm painting an animal it's almost like painting the shadows under all that fur first. Then, when I start painting lighter elements over the underpainting, the strokes really pop out. If anyone happens to walk in and see my painting at this stage when I've painted my reddish brown chipmunk a dark gray they will be completely mystified and I'm sure feel sorry for me, thinking I've completely lost my touch. But almost every painting starts this way.

Blending -- If your paint strokes are left unblended and hard edged your subject will not look realistic. It's fine to leave some strokes unblended for emphasis, but blending them creates subtle variations in color and value and it will look more realistic. You want to avoid flat areas of color. By blending your layers some of the dark value from below will mix with your lighter value above when you add water. Just be careful to use a very slightly damp brush when you blend or you will copletely blend out your strokes. If that happens just repaint the darker layer, repaint your light strokes over it and reblend.

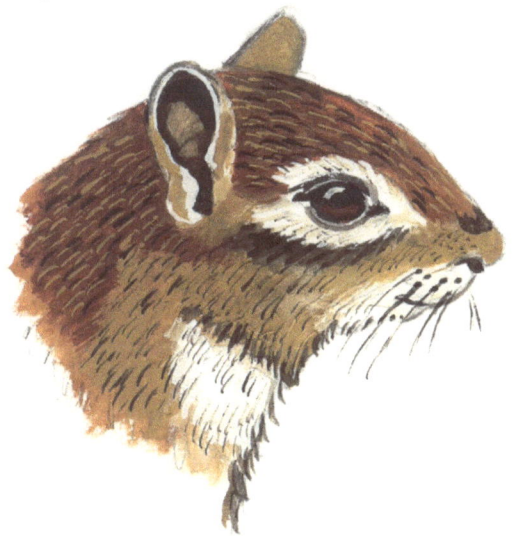

No Underpainting
Unblended

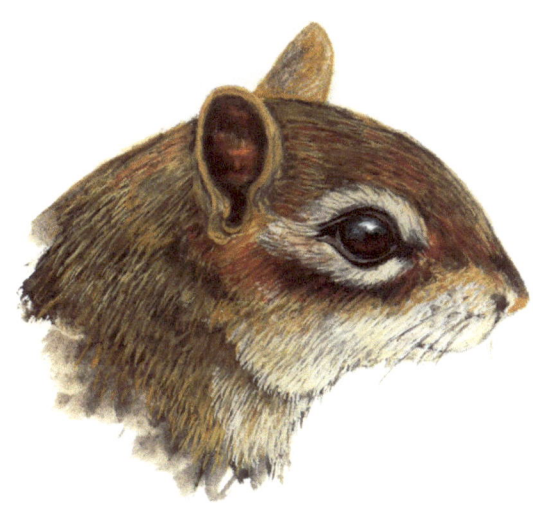

With an Underpainting
and Blended

To blend, dip your brush in water and then run it over a paper towel to remove any excess. Gently move the brush parallel to your strokes to take the hard edges away. This can be time consuming but well worth it in the end.

The following three pages demonstrate how to create the chipmunk head using both underpainting and blending.

Blend Exercise
Eastern Chipmunk Head

Colors Used: Permanent White, Ultramarine Blue, Burnt Umber, Yellow Ochre, Burnt Sienna

(1)

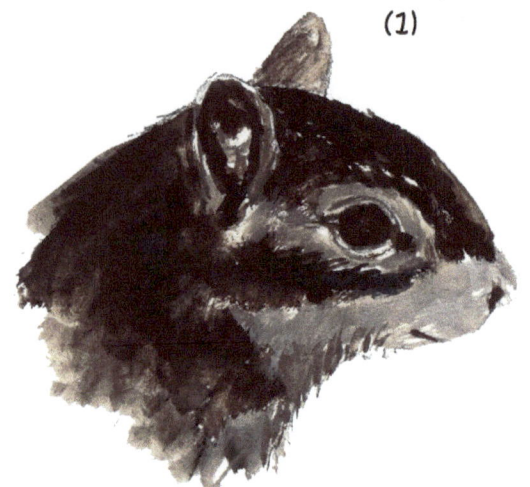

Underpainting -- With a thin mixture of Burnt Umber and Ultramarine Blue, paint the areas that will be the darkest. With White added to this same mixture to make a dark gray, paint the areas that will be white in the finished illustration. Don't worry about getting an even tone. This is an underpainting and most of it will be painted over.

(2)

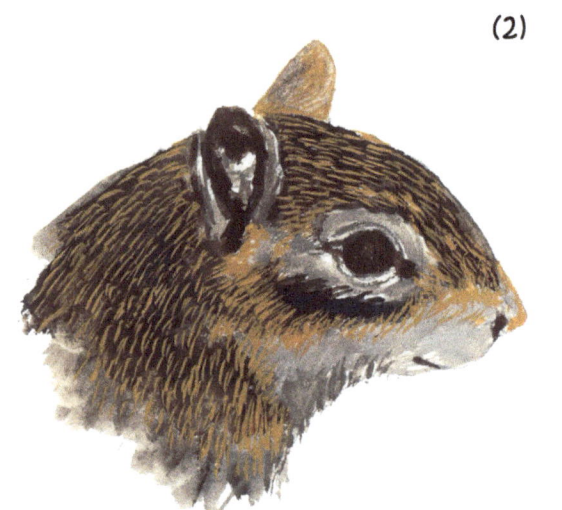

With Yellow Ochre, paint short, thick strokes of gouache going in the direction of the hair pattern. Make your strokes go from the top of the nose all the way back to the shoulders. Don't forget to paint the left ear. Be sure to let the lower layer show through in places

(3)

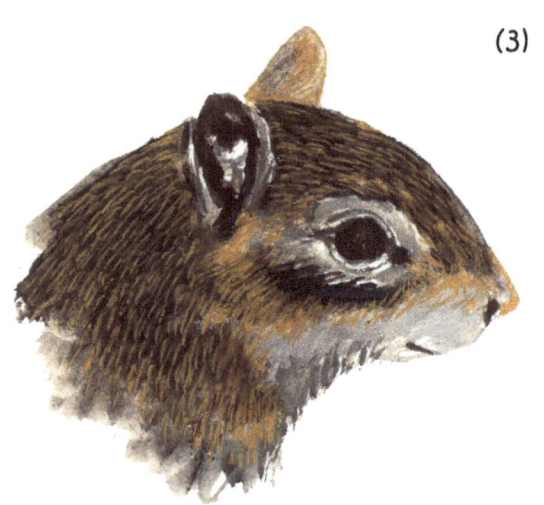

Dip a small brush in water and wipe the excess off on a paper towel. When I paint I always keep a paper towel in my left hand (I'm right handed). Gently run the brush along your Yellow Ochre strokes to blend them in a little. They will become darker when they blend with the lower, darker color.

6

Blend Exercise
Eastern Chipmunk Head

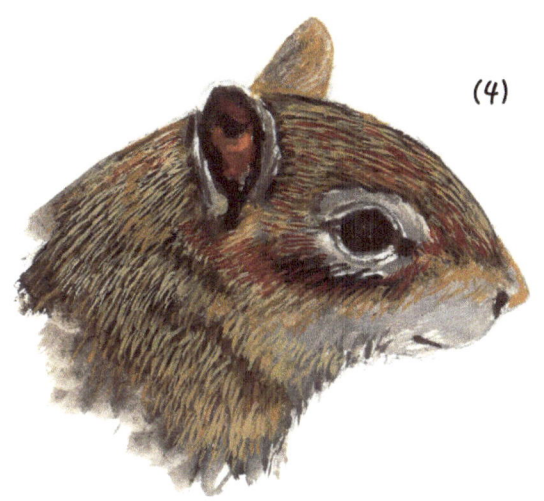

(4)

With White barely tinted with Yellow Ochre, paint another layer of hairs. Also, use Burnt Sienna to add hairs along the forehead and nose and under the left side of the eye. Thin down some Burnt Sienna and paint the inside of the ear.

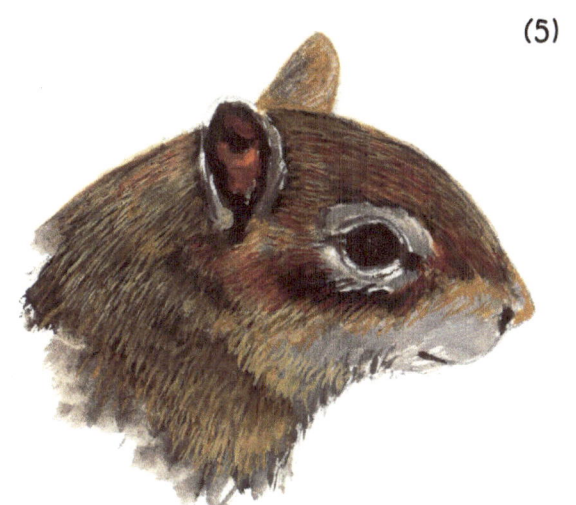

(5)

Dip your brush in clear water again and wipe off the excess. Then gently blend your strokes. As you blend you'll be creating subtle color variations as lower layers combine with the upper layer. Let some of the lower layer show through. Also, take your damp brush and gently soften the outside edges of the chipmunk so it doesn't look pasted on the paper.

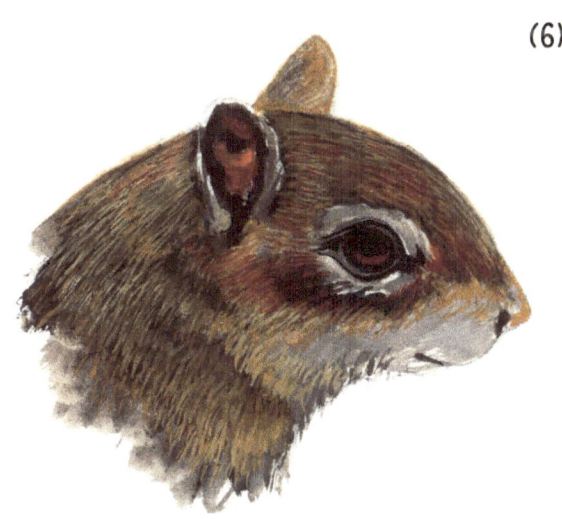

(6)

Eye -- With your darkest value of Burnt Umber and Ultramarine Blue mix, refine the shape of the eye. Add White to the mixture to make a medium value gray and paint the narrow lines on the rims of the chipmunk's eye. Also, use Burnt Sienna to paint a semicircle on the lower half of the pupil of the eye.

Blend Exercise
Eastern Chipmunk Head

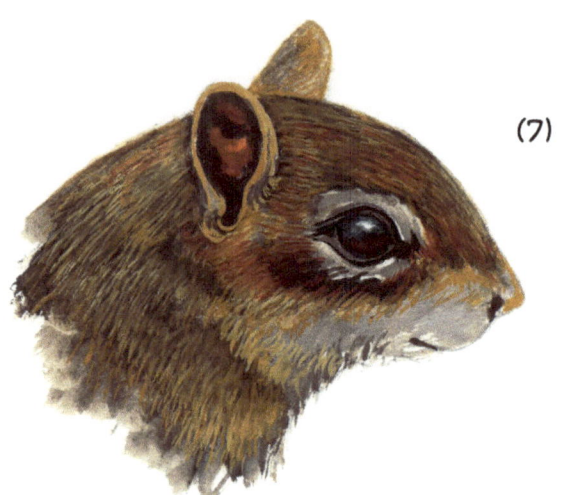

(7) Eye -- Gently blend in the Burnt Sienna in the eye until you can barely see it. Using White mixed with Ultramarine Blue, paint a highlight in the eye and blend the edges. Then use pure White to dot in a sharp highlight.
Ear -- With Yellow Ochre mixed with a little White, paint the outside rim of the right ear.

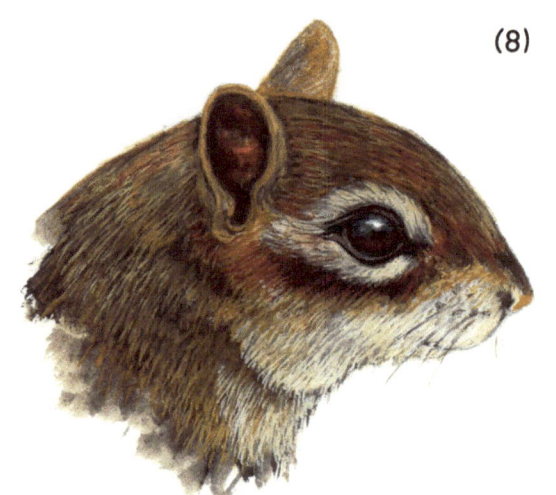

(8) With pure White, paint in the hairs above and below the eye and on the muzzle and chest. Gently blend them a little. They'll pick up some of the color from below and become darker. If you lose too much of the white just add more. With Burnt Umber, paint a little dark spot on top of the nose. Blend the Yellow Ochre in the edges of the ear and the shadow area inside the ear.
Whiskers -- With Burnt Umber tinted with White paint in the little dots that the whiskers grow out of. Blend them. With your tiniest brush use the same Burnt Umber and White mixture to lightly paint in the whiskers. Then use a little White to paint a thin line on the top edge of each whisker hair.

The key to learning good underpainting and blending techniques is practice, practice, practice! It will then become second nature to you as you plan your own works.

White Footed Mouse

Peromyscus leucopus

Colors Used: Permanent White, Burnt Umber, Ultramarine Blue,
Olive Green, Brilliant Yellow, Burnt Sienna, Brilliant Violet, Yellow Ochre

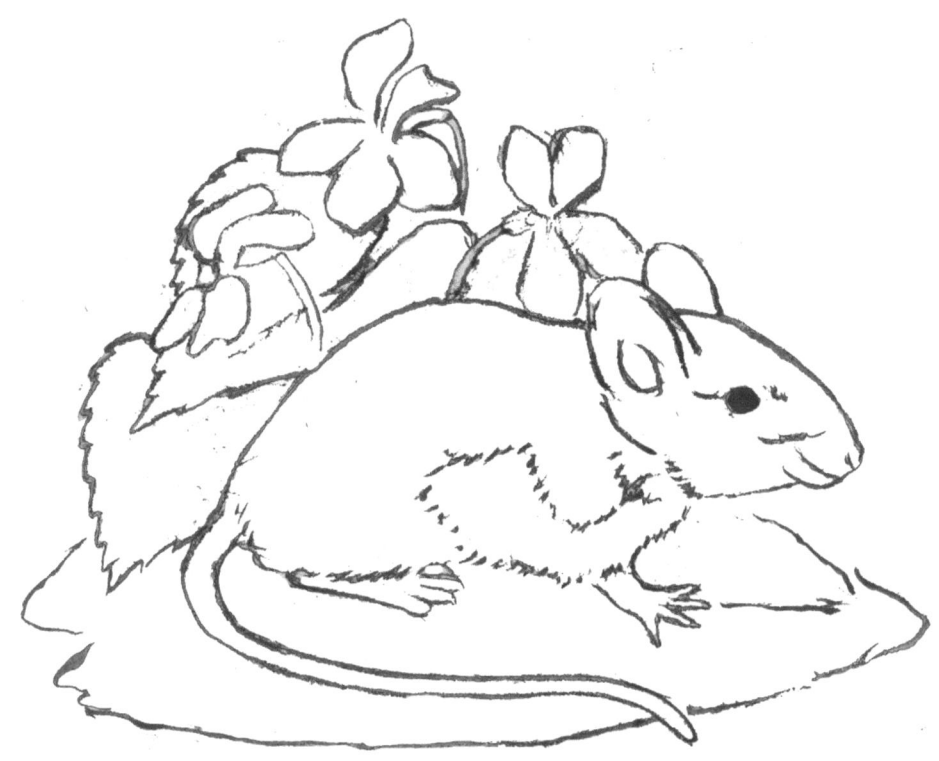

Use this sheet to transfer the image to your sheet of hot press
watercolor paper or illustration board.

White Footed Mouse

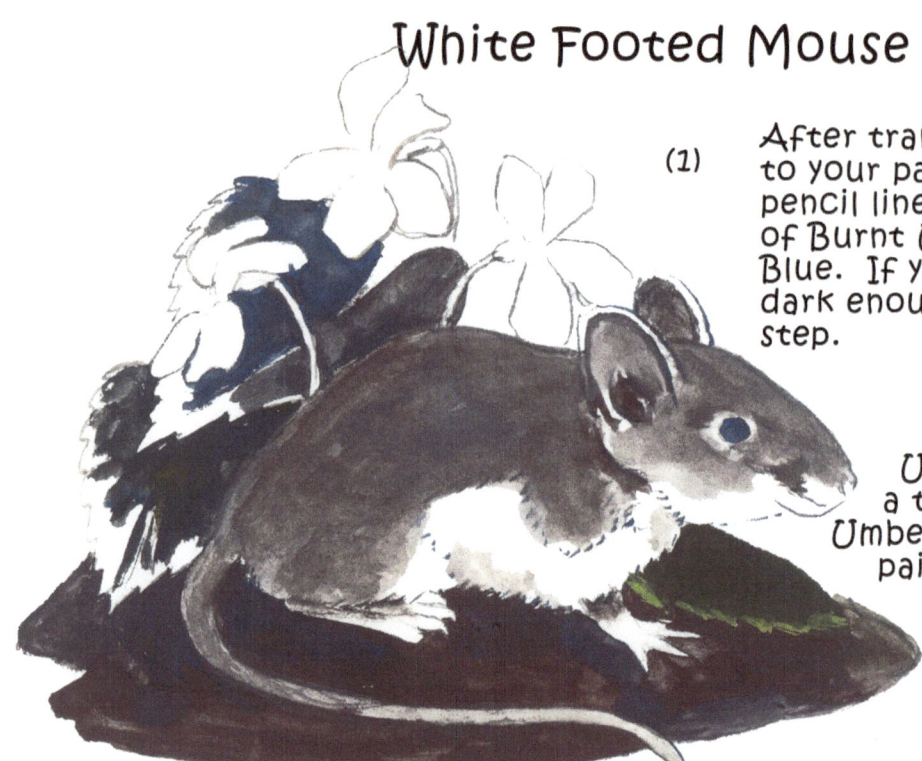

(1) After transferring your drawing to your paper, go over your pencil lines with a dark mixture of Burnt Umber and Ultramarine Blue. If your pencil lines are dark enough you can skip this step.

Underpainting -- With a thin mixture of Burnt Umber and Ultramarine Blue, paint the ground, leaves and mouse (in the darker areas).

Don't worry about getting an even tone. This is just an underpainting and it will be much darker than your finished work.

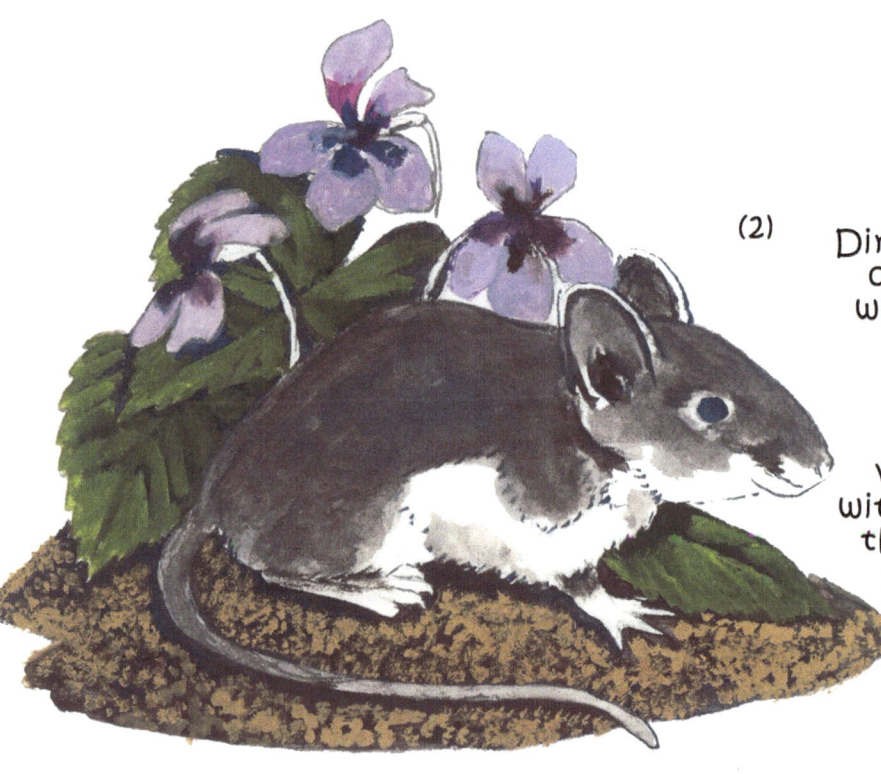

(2) Dirt - With Yellow Ochre, dot on small areas of gouache where the dirt will be. The paint should be a little thick.

Leaves -- With a medium value of Olive Green mixed with Brilliant Yellow, paint over the rest of the white on the leaves. Also, make broad strokes of your green mixture in the shadow areas of the leaves.

Flowers -- Mix Brilliant Violet with Ultramarine Blue and paint the dark centers of the flowers. Add the same mixture to white and paint the rest of the petals.

10

White Footed Mouse

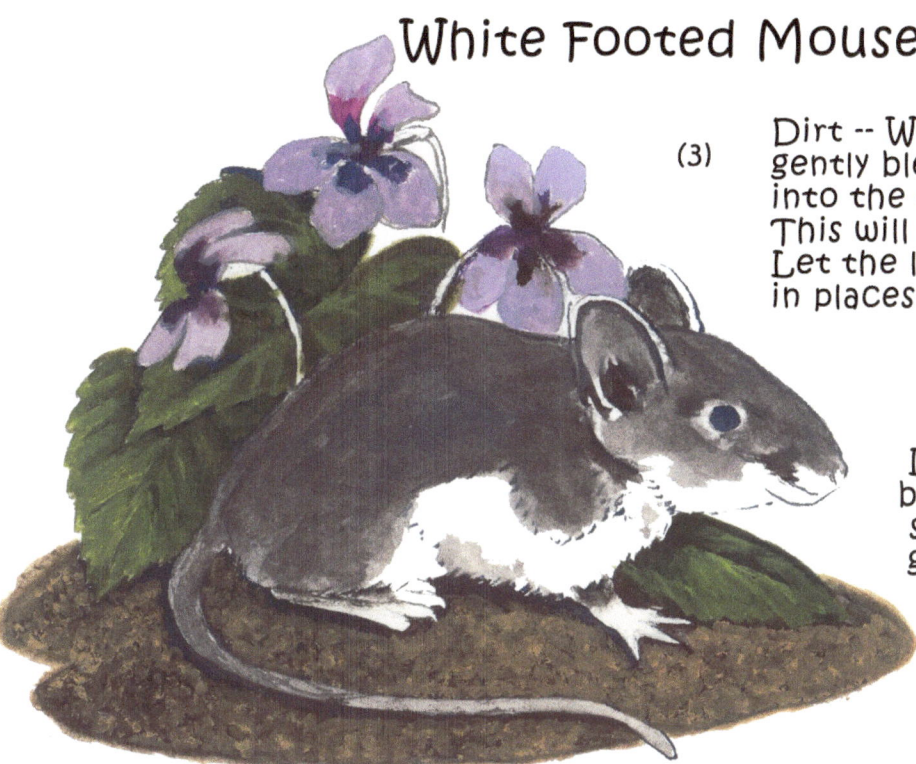

(3) Dirt -- With a damp brush, gently blend the Yellow Ochre into the dark underpainting. This will smooth out your strokes. Let the lower layer show through in places.

Leaves -- With a damp brush, smooth out the strokes on the leaves, going from the center vein outward to the edges of the leaves.

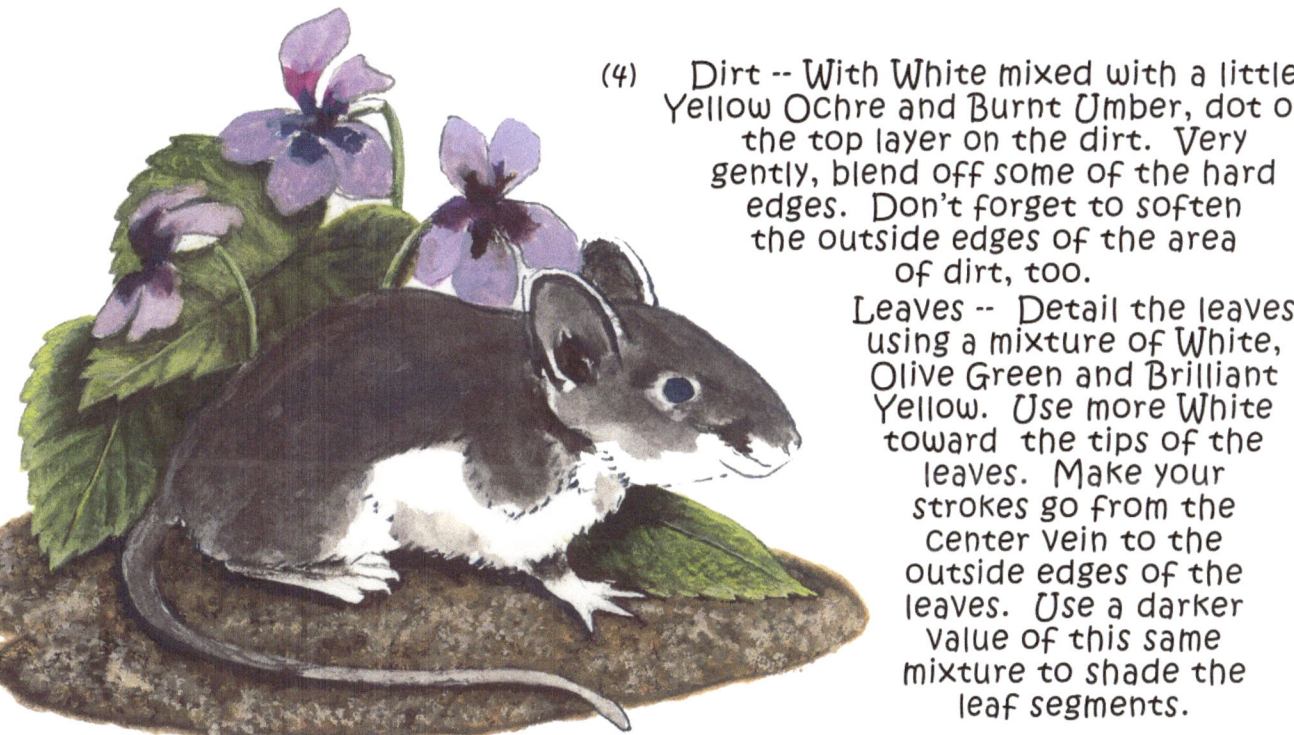

(4) Dirt -- With White mixed with a little Yellow Ochre and Burnt Umber, dot on the top layer on the dirt. Very gently, blend off some of the hard edges. Don't forget to soften the outside edges of the area of dirt, too.

Leaves -- Detail the leaves using a mixture of White, Olive Green and Brilliant Yellow. Use more White toward the tips of the leaves. Make your strokes go from the center vein to the outside edges of the leaves. Use a darker value of this same mixture to shade the leaf segments.

Use White mixed with Brilliant Yellow to paint a very thin line for the center vein. Use Burnt Umber mixed with Ultramarine Blue to restate some of the darkest shadows. With a slightly damp brush, blend off the hard edges of your strokes. Paint the flower stems light green with a little shading on the left side made by mixing Olive Green and Ultramarine Blue.

White Footed Mouse

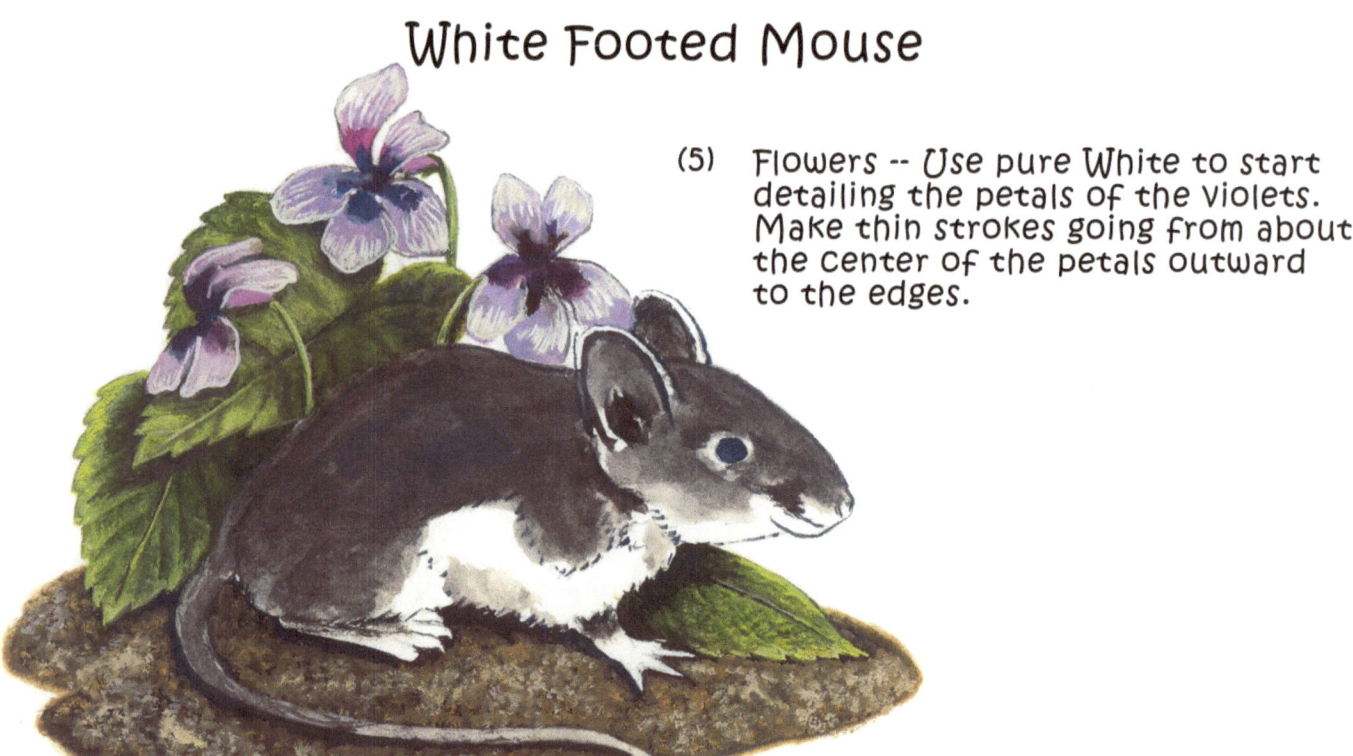

(5) Flowers -- Use pure White to start detailing the petals of the violets. Make thin strokes going from about the center of the petals outward to the edges.

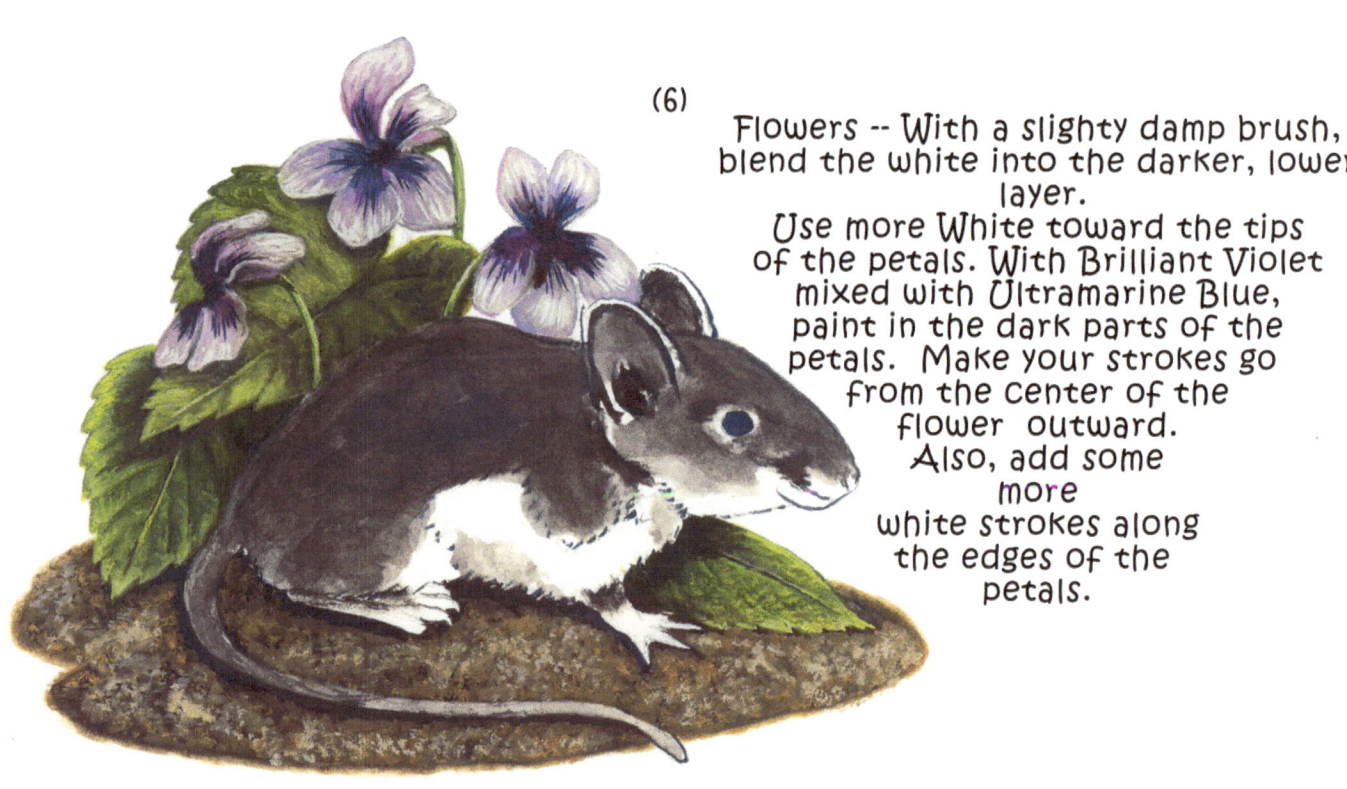

(6) Flowers -- With a slighty damp brush, blend the white into the darker, lower layer.
Use more White toward the tips of the petals. With Brilliant Violet mixed with Ultramarine Blue, paint in the dark parts of the petals. Make your strokes go from the center of the flower outward.
Also, add some more white strokes along the edges of the petals.

White Footed Mouse

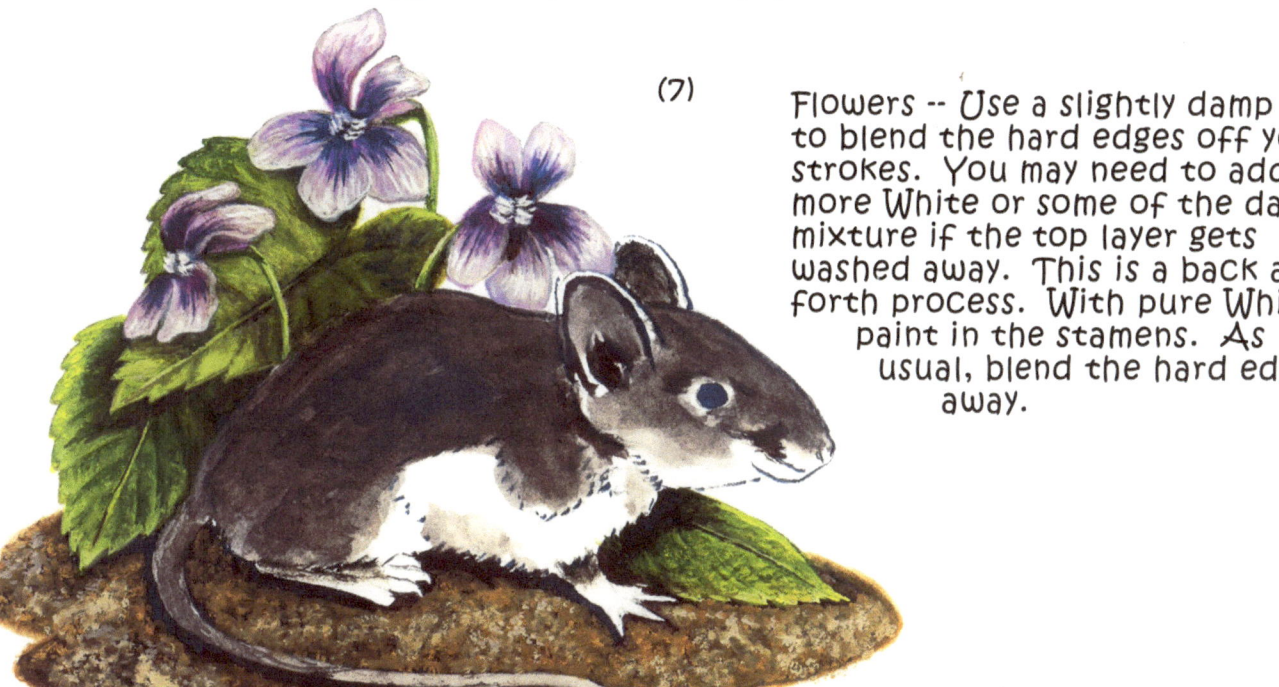

(7)

Flowers -- Use a slightly damp brush to blend the hard edges off your strokes. You may need to add more White or some of the dark mixture if the top layer gets washed away. This is a back and forth process. With pure White paint in the stamens. As usual, blend the hard edges away.

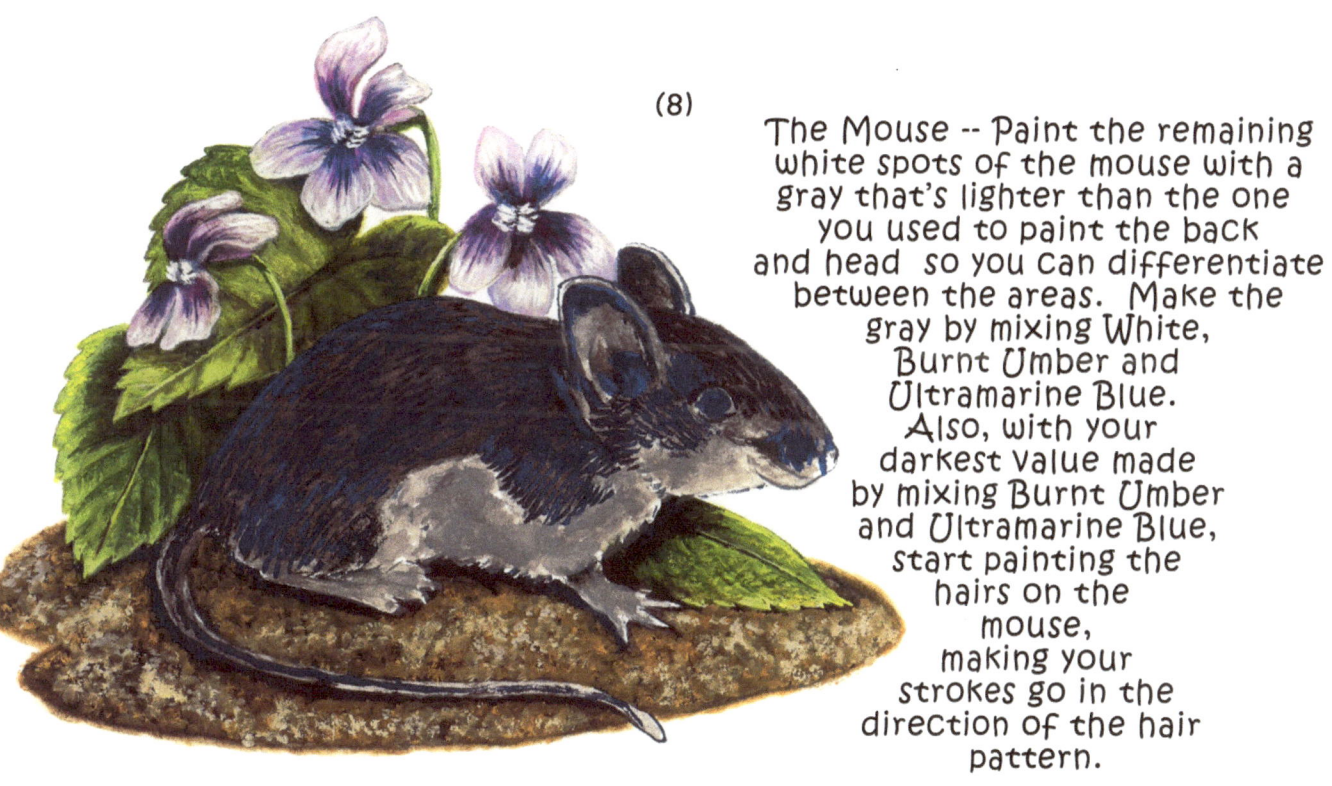

(8)

The Mouse -- Paint the remaining white spots of the mouse with a gray that's lighter than the one you used to paint the back and head so you can differentiate between the areas. Make the gray by mixing White, Burnt Umber and Ultramarine Blue. Also, with your darkest value made by mixing Burnt Umber and Ultramarine Blue, start painting the hairs on the mouse, making your strokes go in the direction of the hair pattern.

White Footed Mouse

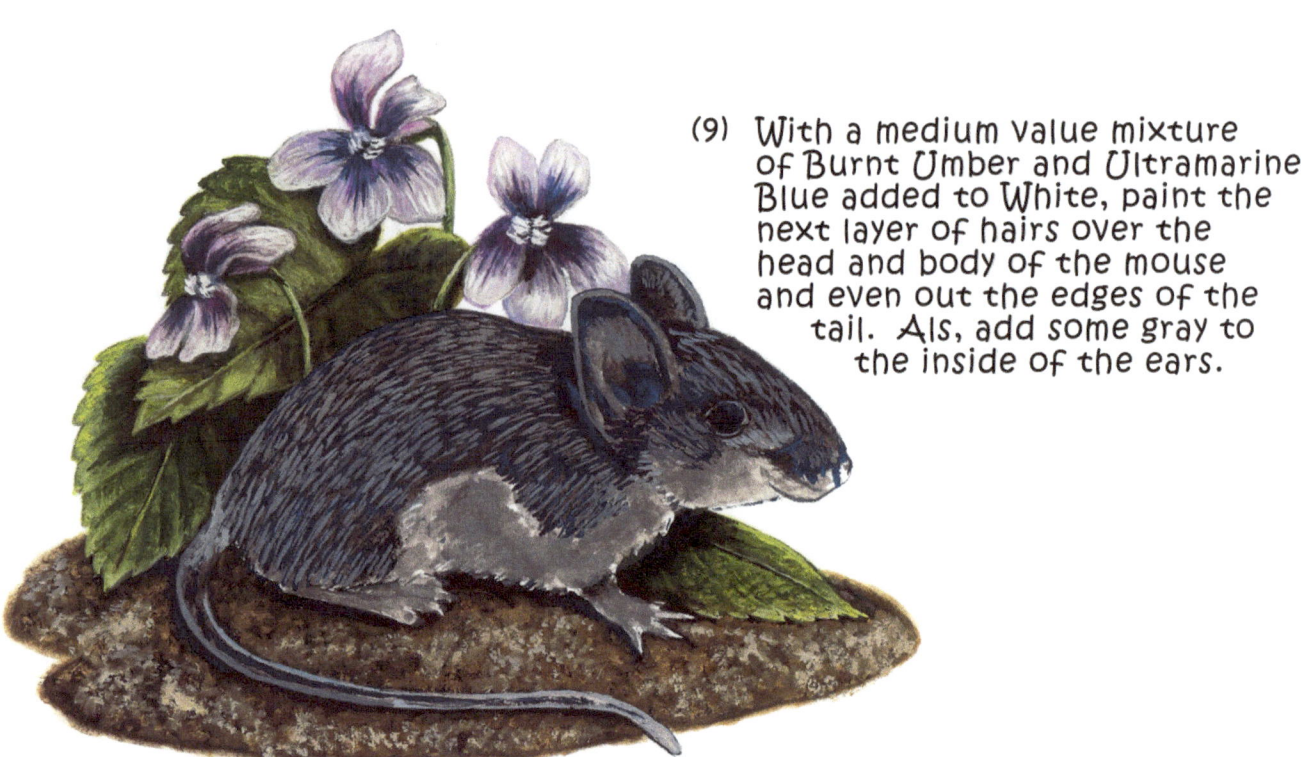

(9) With a medium value mixture of Burnt Umber and Ultramarine Blue added to White, paint the next layer of hairs over the head and body of the mouse and even out the edges of the tail. Als, add some gray to the inside of the ears.

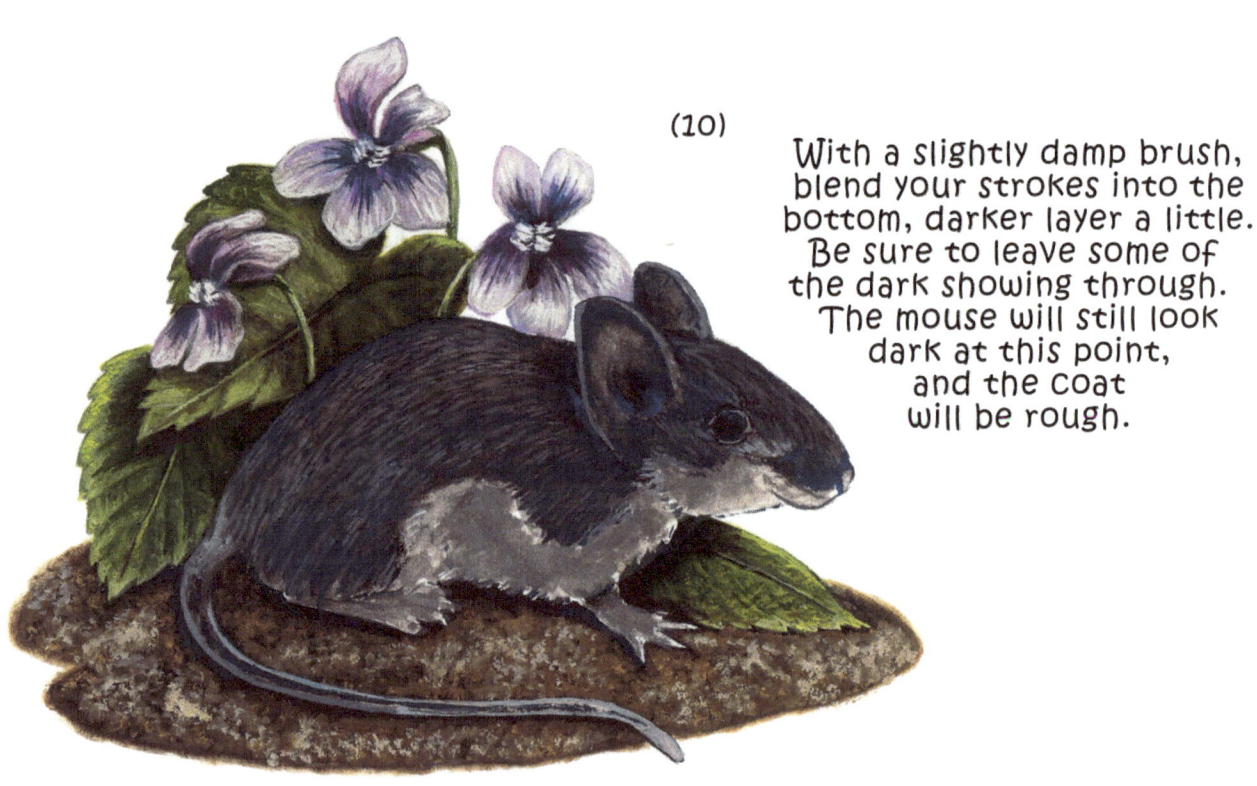

(10) With a slightly damp brush, blend your strokes into the bottom, darker layer a little. Be sure to leave some of the dark showing through. The mouse will still look dark at this point, and the coat will be rough.

White Footed Mouse

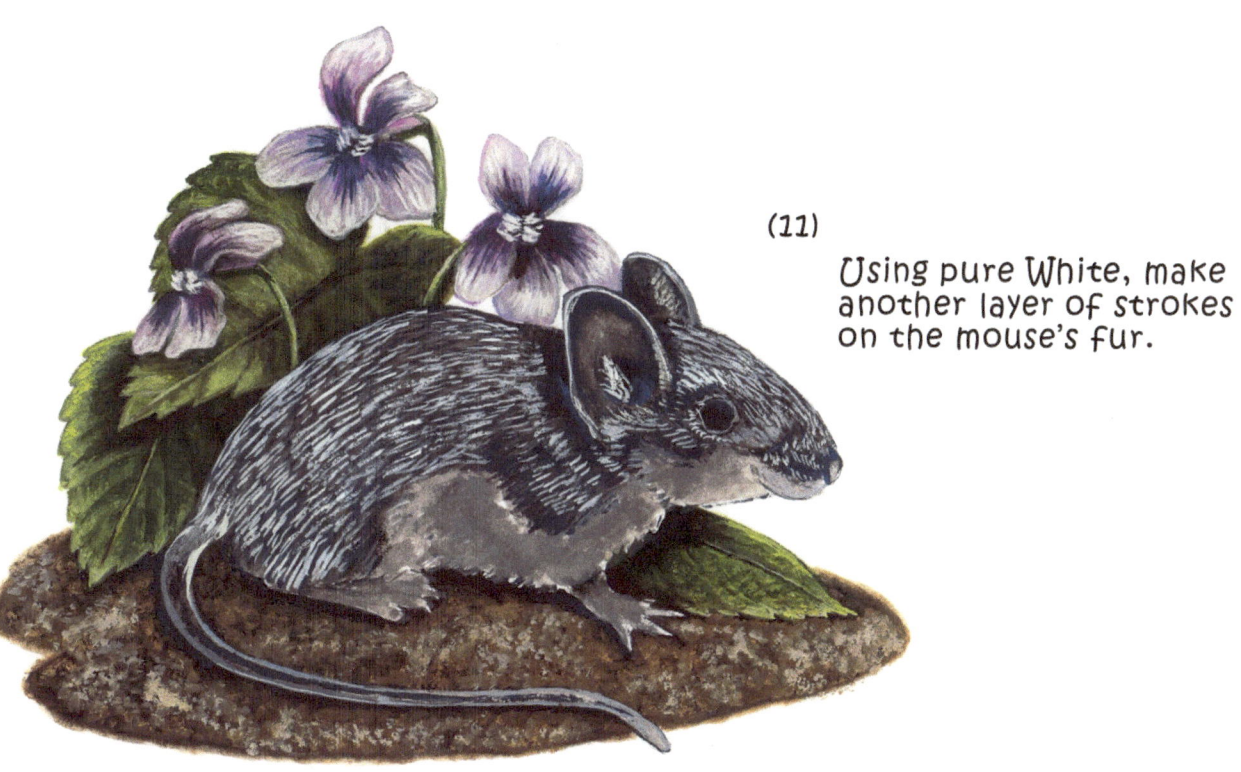

(11)
Using pure White, make another layer of strokes on the mouse's fur.

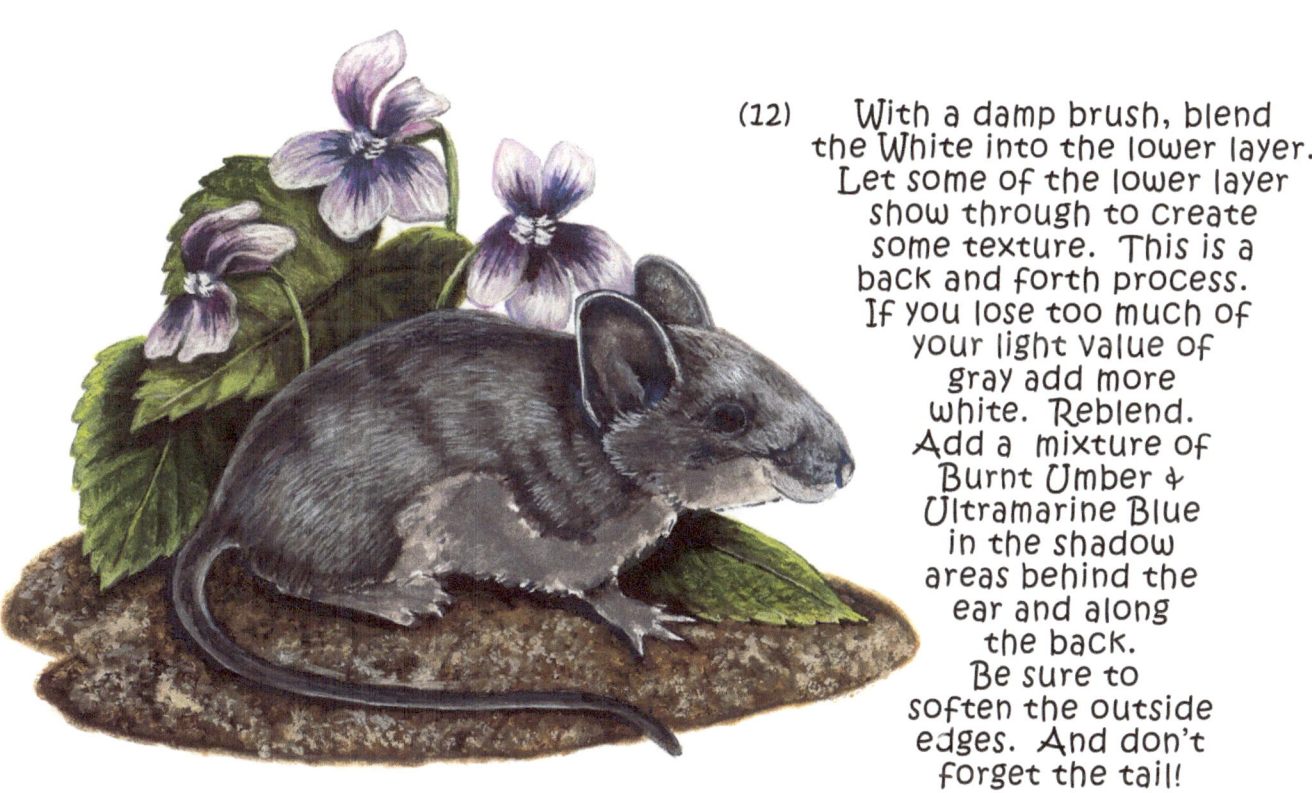

(12) With a damp brush, blend the White into the lower layer. Let some of the lower layer show through to create some texture. This is a back and forth process. If you lose too much of your light value of gray add more white. Reblend. Add a mixture of Burnt Umber & Ultramarine Blue in the shadow areas behind the ear and along the back. Be sure to soften the outside edges. And don't forget the tail!

White Footed Mouse

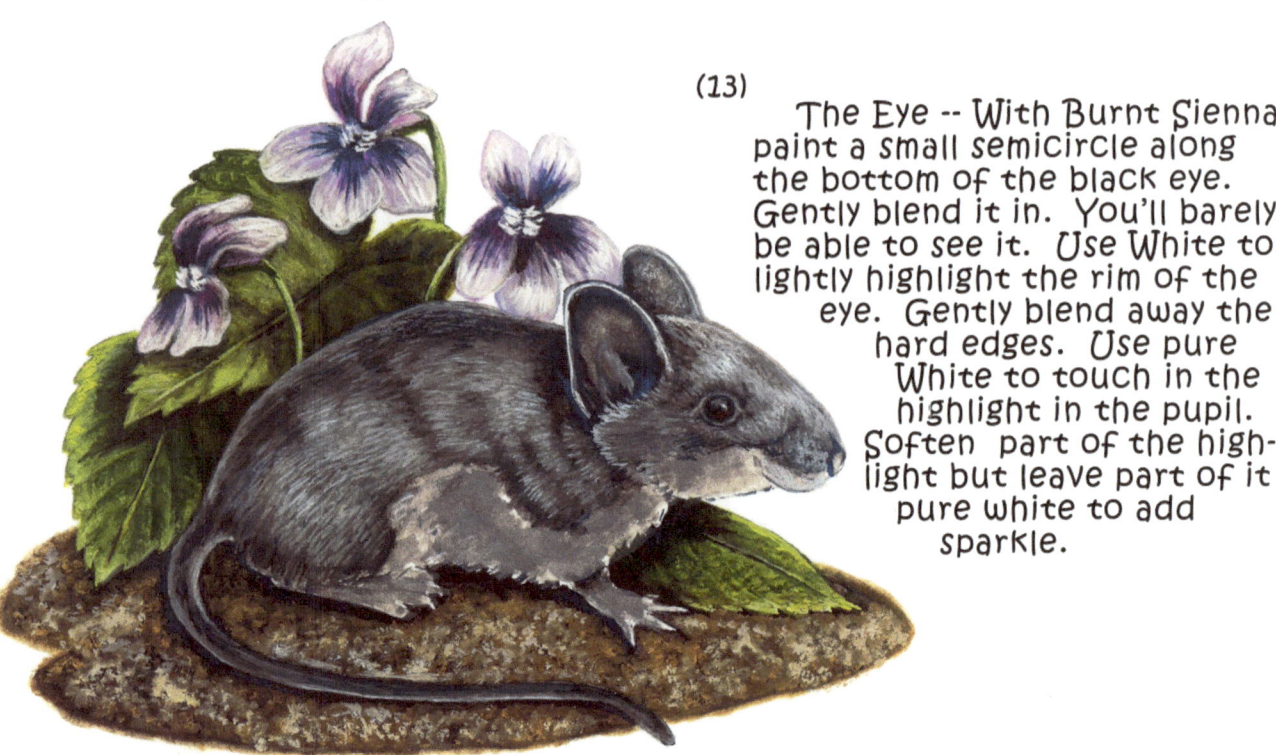

(13)

The Eye -- With Burnt Sienna paint a small semicircle along the bottom of the black eye. Gently blend it in. You'll barely be able to see it. Use White to lightly highlight the rim of the eye. Gently blend away the hard edges. Use pure White to touch in the highlight in the pupil. Soften part of the highlight but leave part of it pure white to add sparkle.

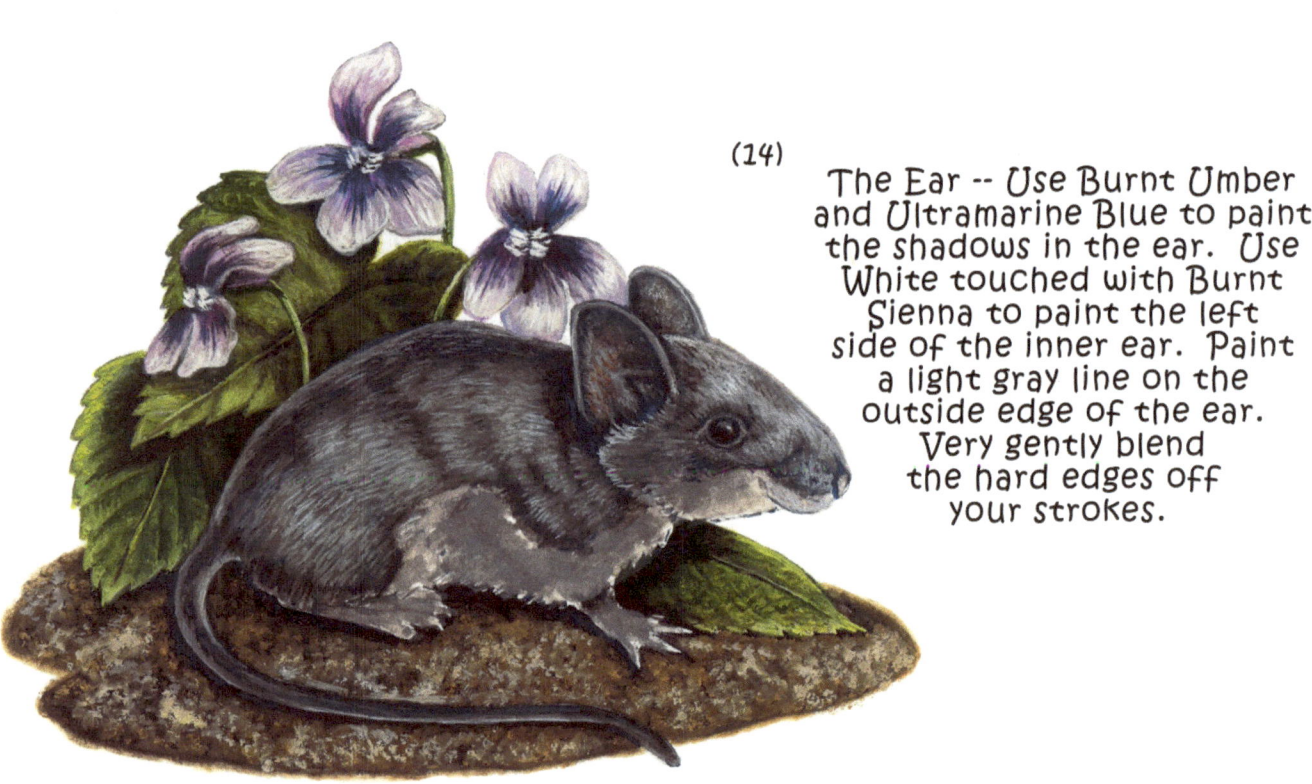

(14)

The Ear -- Use Burnt Umber and Ultramarine Blue to paint the shadows in the ear. Use White touched with Burnt Sienna to paint the left side of the inner ear. Paint a light gray line on the outside edge of the ear. Very gently blend the hard edges off your strokes.

White Footed Mouse

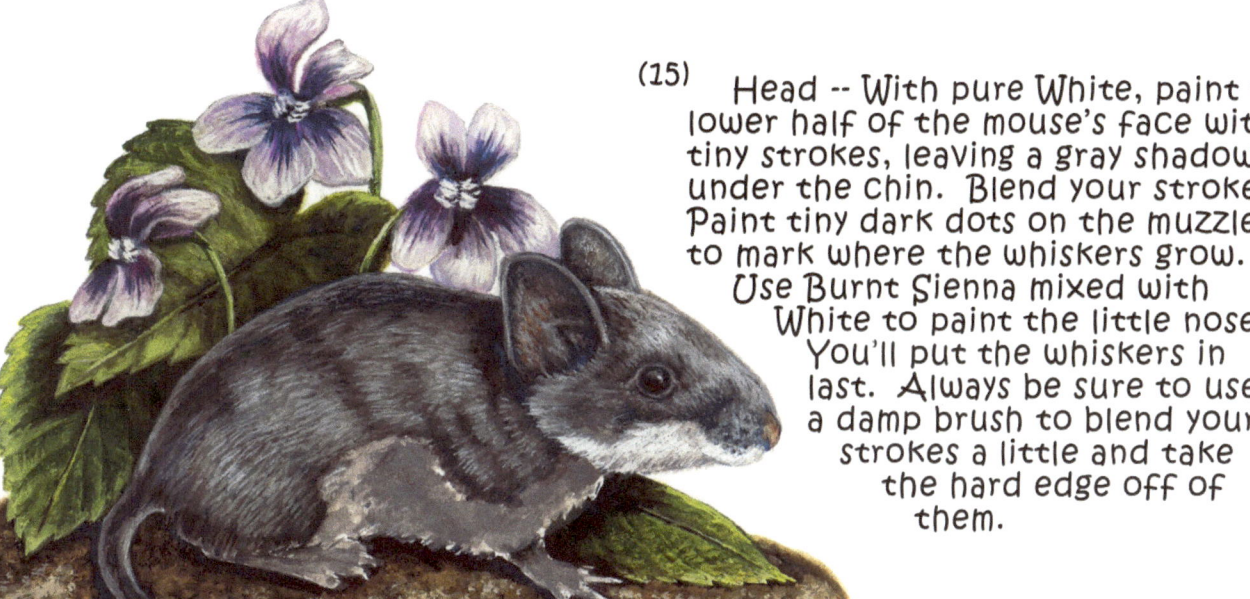

(15) Head -- With pure White, paint the lower half of the mouse's face with tiny strokes, leaving a gray shadow under the chin. Blend your strokes. Paint tiny dark dots on the muzzle to mark where the whiskers grow. Use Burnt Sienna mixed with White to paint the little nose. You'll put the whiskers in last. Always be sure to use a damp brush to blend your strokes a little and take the hard edge off of them.

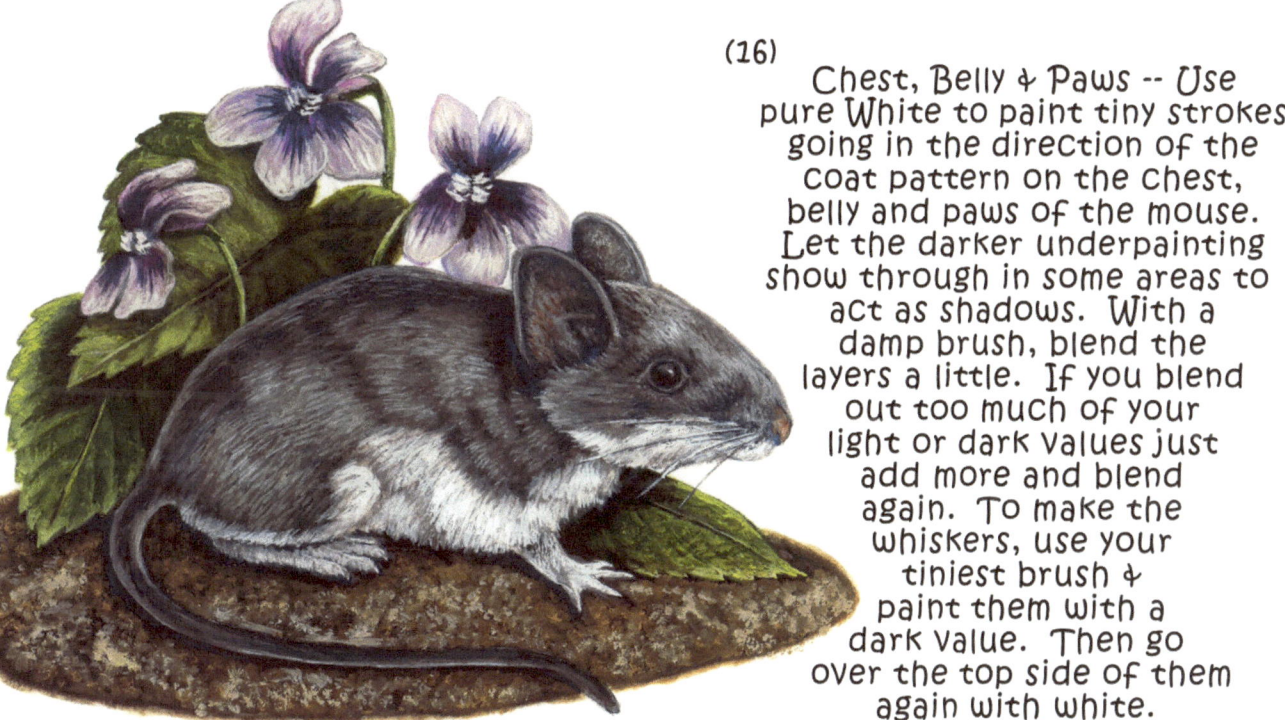

(16) Chest, Belly & Paws -- Use pure White to paint tiny strokes going in the direction of the coat pattern on the chest, belly and paws of the mouse. Let the darker underpainting show through in some areas to act as shadows. With a damp brush, blend the layers a little. If you blend out too much of your light or dark values just add more and blend again. To make the whiskers, use your tiniest brush & paint them with a dark value. Then go over the top side of them again with white.

It's always a good practice to put your painting down for a few days after you think it may be finished and then look at it again from a fresh perspective later on. Make any needed changes to values or detailing before you call it complete!

Eastern Chipmunk

Tamias striatus

Colors Used: Permanent White, Burnt Umber, Ultramarine Blue, Olive Green, Brilliant Yellow, Marigold Yellow, Burnt Sienna Yellow Ochre

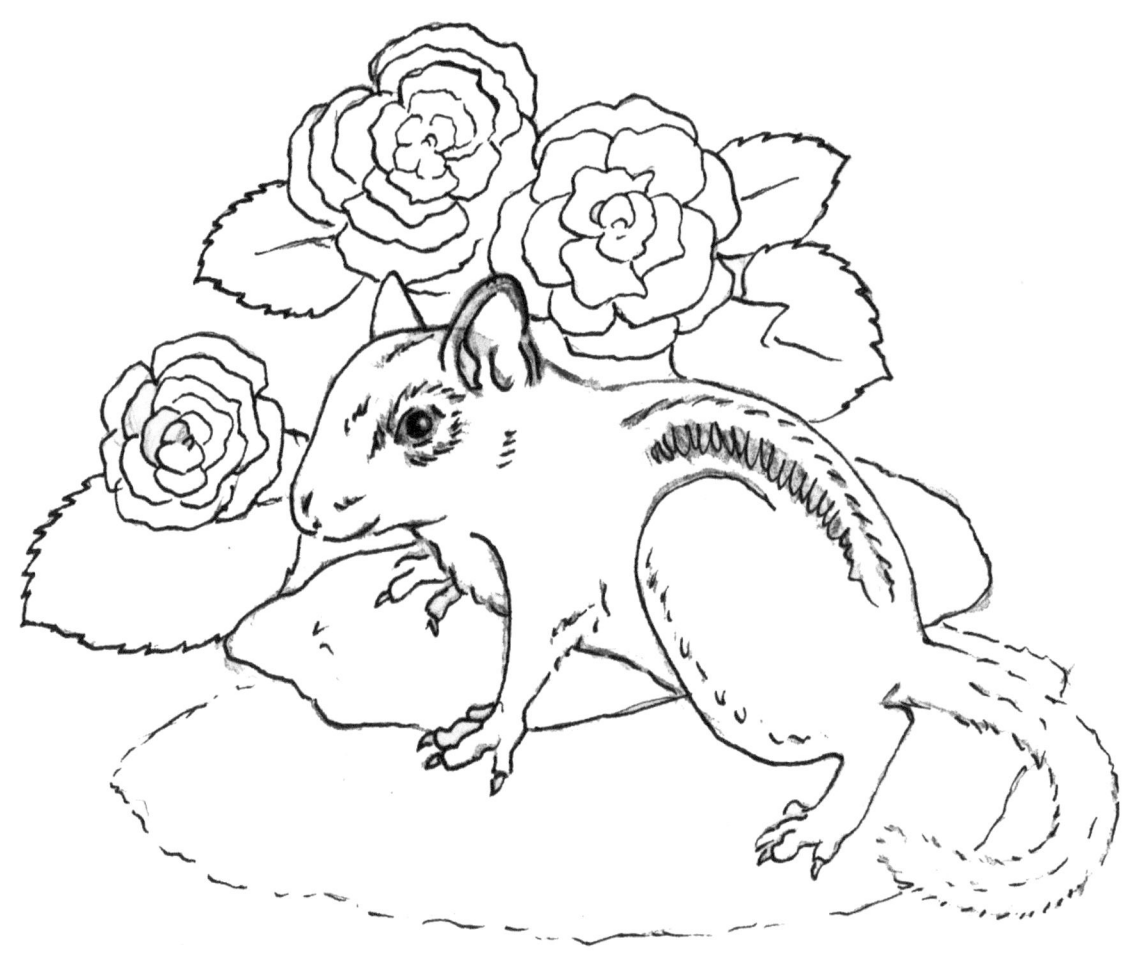

Use this sheet to transfer the image to your sheet of hot press watercolor paper or illustration board.

Eastern Chipmunk

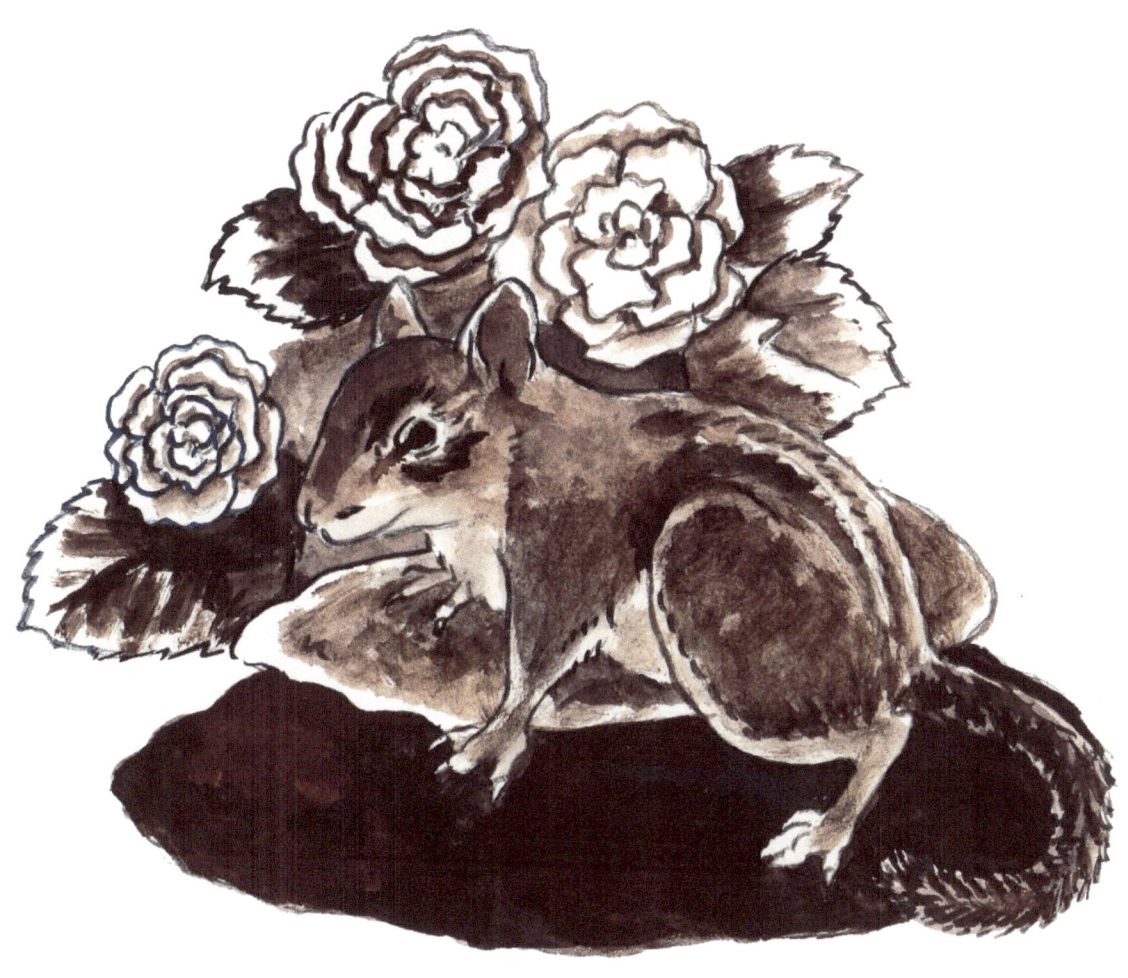

(1)

 After transferring the drawing to your paper use a dark mixture of Burnt Umber and Ultramarine Blue to paint over your lines so they don't get lost when you start layering on the gouache. If your lines are dark enough you can skip this step.

The Underpainting -- With the same dark mixture of Burnt Umber and Ultramarine Blue, paint the underpainting. This lowest layer is thinned with water. Don't worry about getting an even tone. This is just the underpainting and it will be much darker than the finished illustration.

Eastern Chipmunk

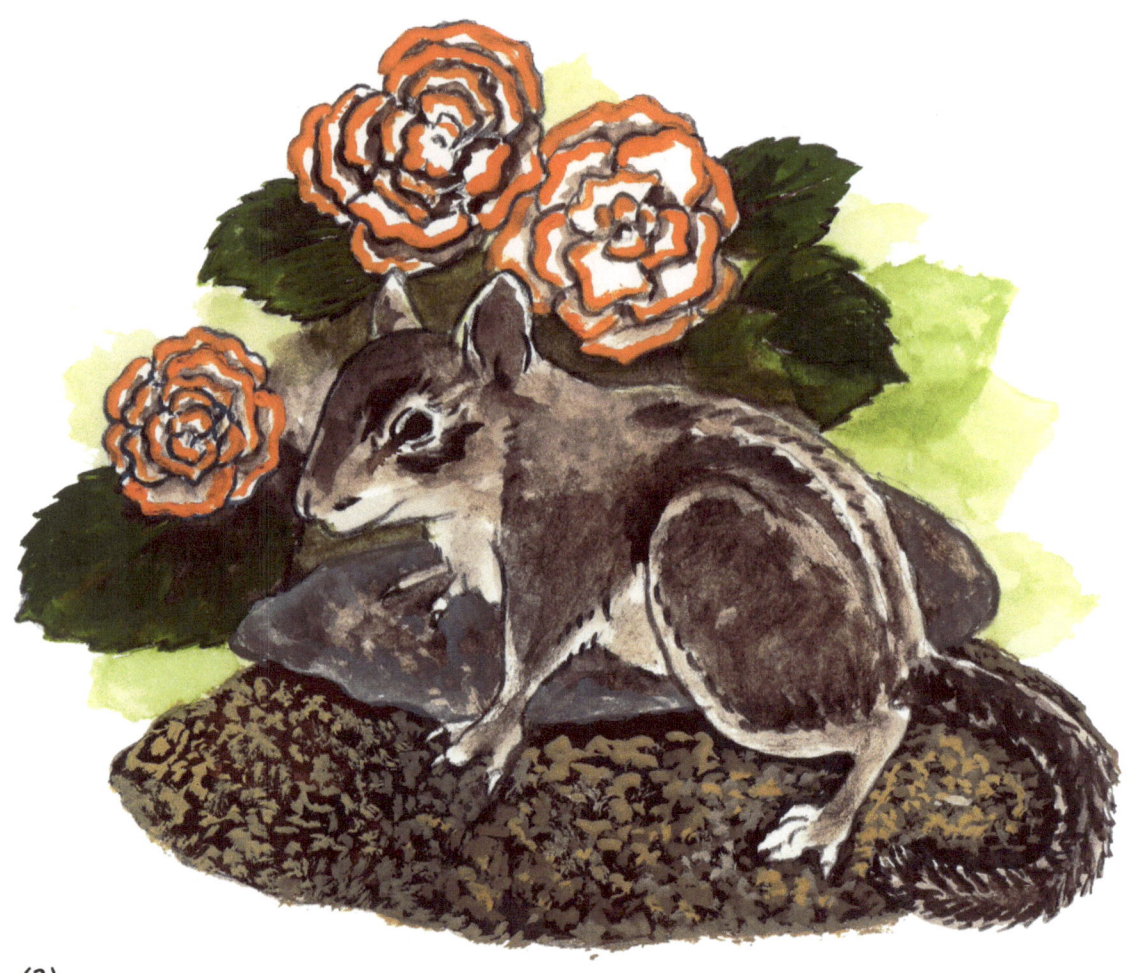

(2)

Leaves -- With Olive Green, paint a layer of gouache on the leaves. With watered down Olive Green paint in some vague, indistinct leaves in the background, around the outside of the plant.

Rock - With a medium mixture of White, Burnt Umber and Ultramarine Blue, paint the rest of the white spaces on the rock.

Dirt -- Mix White with Burnt Umber and Yellow Ochre to make a medium value. With the tip of your brush, dot the gouache over the dark layer you painted before. Don't completely cover the bottom layer. Later on, when you begin to blend, the layer will form mottled gradations.

Flowers -- With Marigold Yellow, paint the edges of the petals on the flowers.

It looks a little strange, right? Just remember -- this is only the underpainting.

Eastern Chipmunk

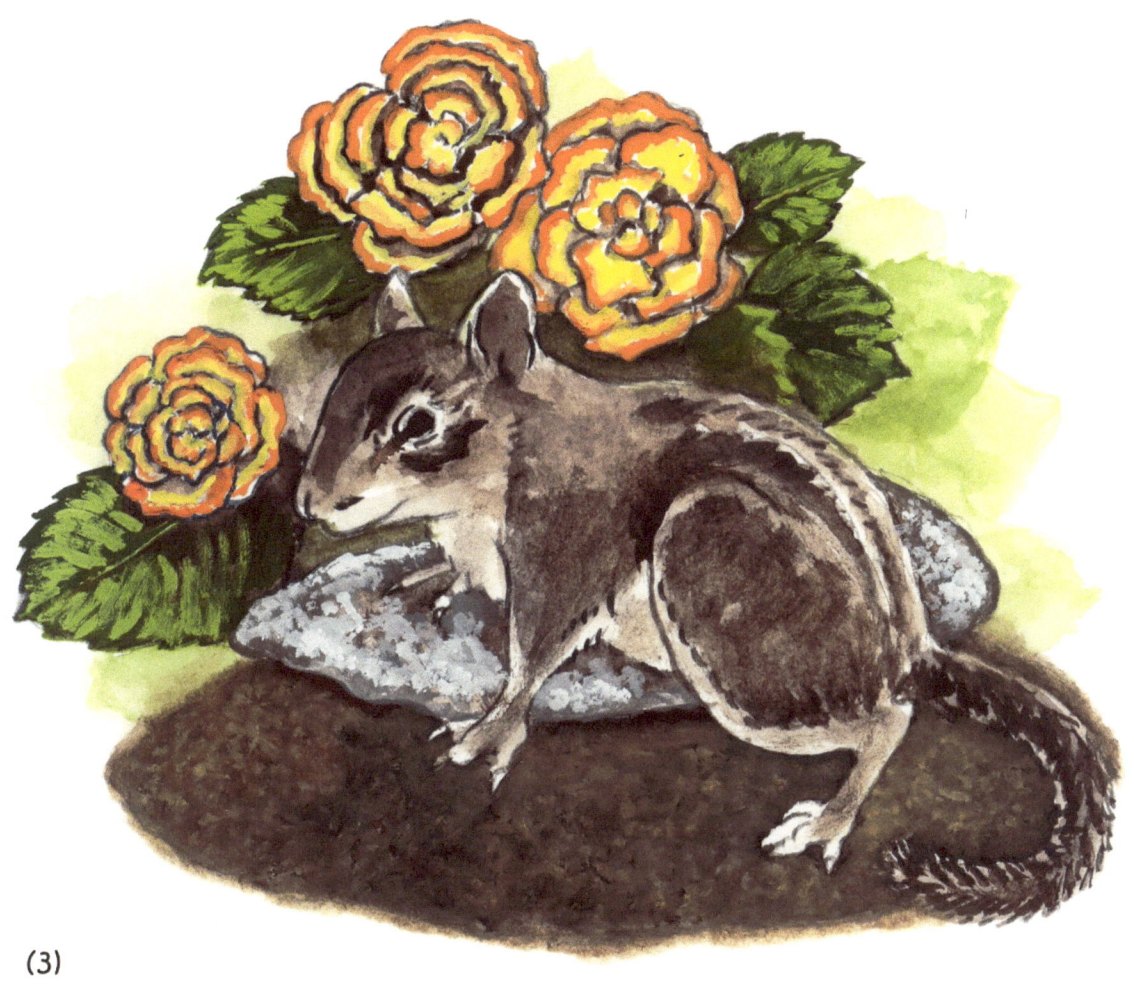

(3)

   Leaves -- With a light value of White mixed with Brilliant Yellow and Olive Green, roughly paint in the next layer of gouache on the leaves. Make your strokes go from the center vein outward to the edges.

Dirt -- With a very slightly damp brush, gently blend together the layers you painted previously to make subtle gradations. If you use too much water you'll blend too much and end up with a flat area of color. If this happens just start over -- paint a dark lower layer with a lighter layer dotted on top. Reblend. Also, soften all the outside edges with the same slightly damp brush.

Rock -- With White mixed with a tiny bit of your Burnt Umber and Ultramarine Blue mixture, use the tip of your brush to make texture on the rock.

Flowers -- With White mixed with Brilliant Yellow, paint the remaining white areas of the flowers.

Eastern Chipmunk

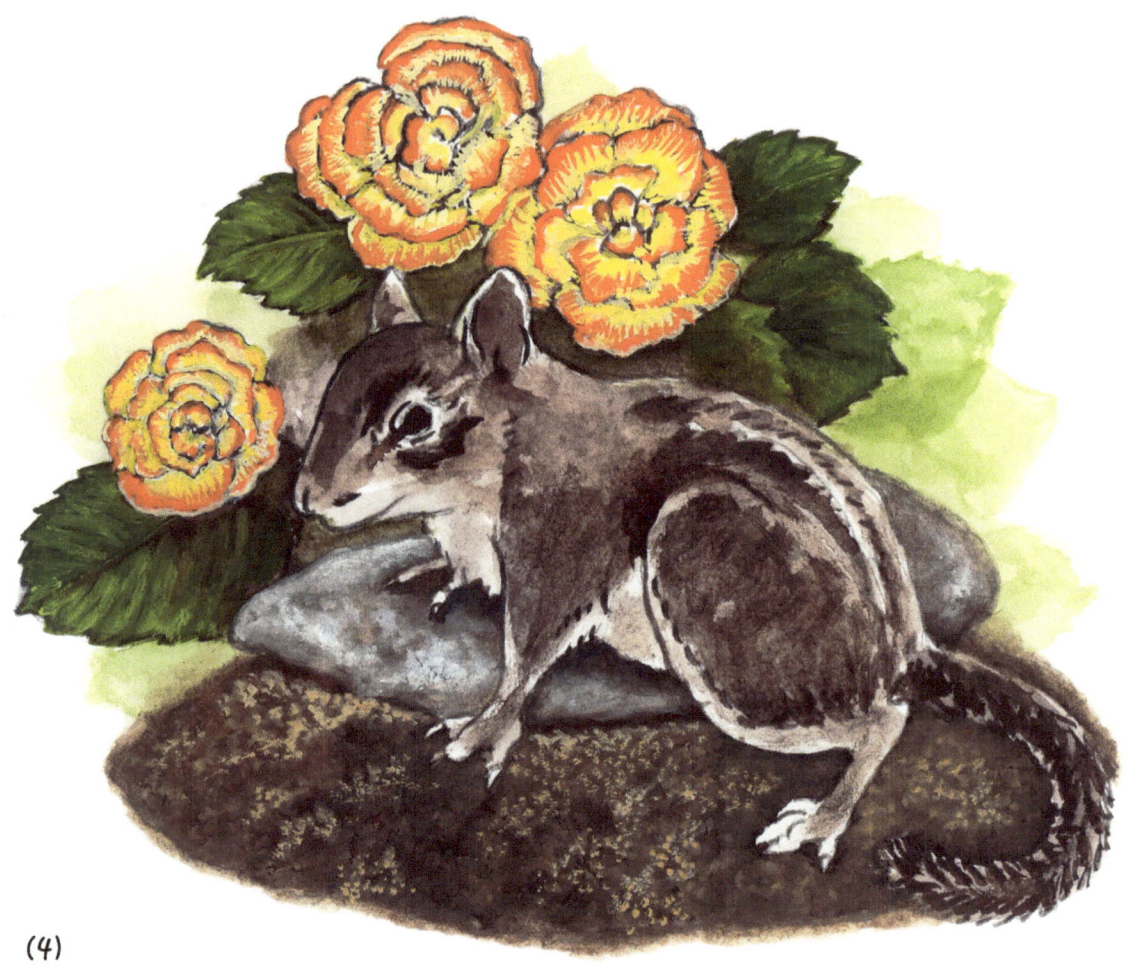

(4)

Leaves -- With a very slightly damp brush, blend the light value into the darker one. Try to keep your strokes going from the center vein to the outside edge.

Dirt -- With a very light mixture of White and Yellow Ochre, finish texturing the dirt by adding little dots of paint with the tip of your brush. With a damp brush very gently blend the edges of the dots into the background color.

Rock -- Blend the light value into the dark. Using a dark mixture of Burnt Umber and Ultramarine Blue paint shadows under the paw and belly. Gently blend the edge of the shadows to soften them.

Flowers -- Begin detailing the petals. Use White mixed with Brilliant Yellow to paint strokes going from the center of the petal outward to about halfway along. Then use Marigold Yellow and paint strokes going from the edge of the petal to the center, about half-way along. Cover up the dark lines outlining the petals.

Eastern Chipmunk

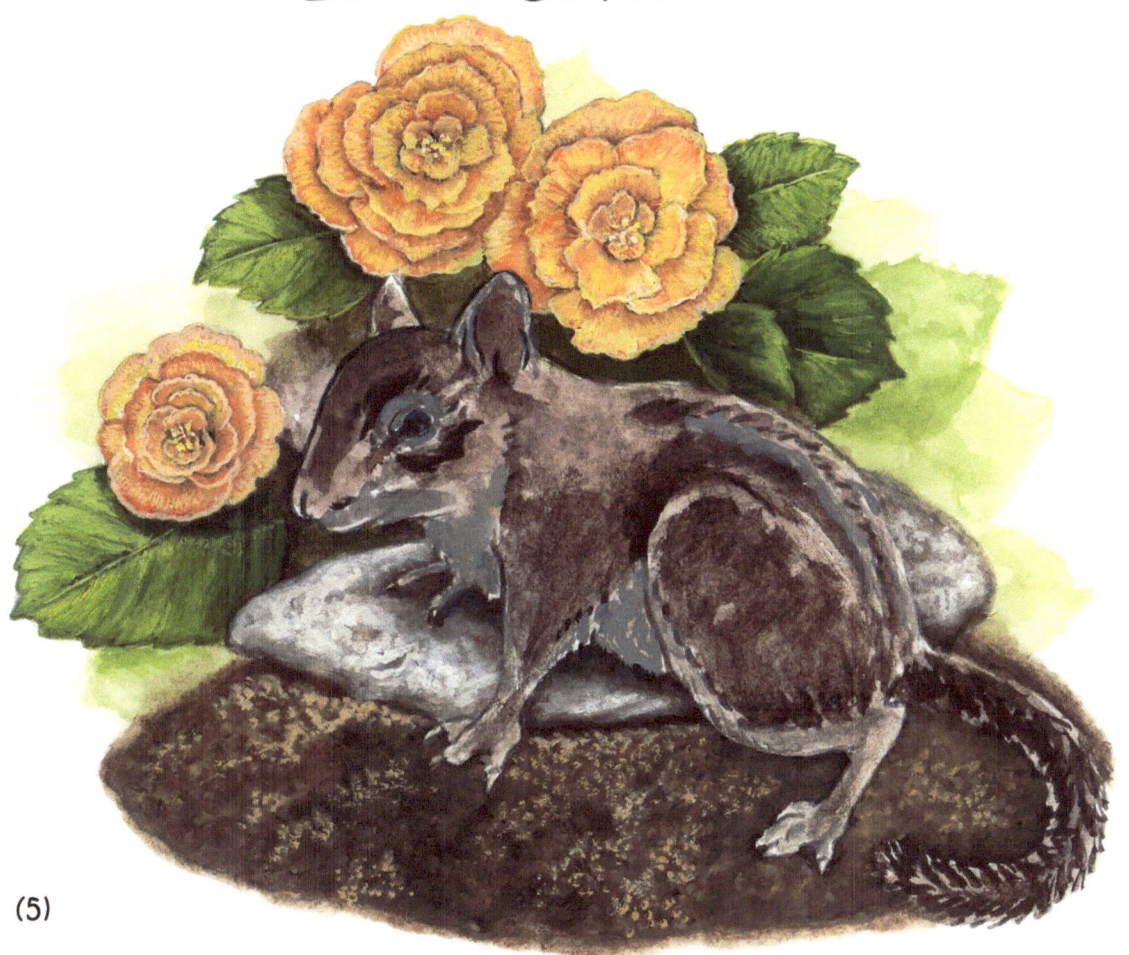

(5)

Leaves -- To finish detailing the leaves use a mixture of White, Brilliant Yellow and Olive Green and paint the top layer of gouache. Always make your strokes go from the center vein to the outside edge. Gently blend the colors. You will probably have to add more of the light value toward the tips of the leaves and blend again. Also, add a mixture of Burnt Umber and Ultramarine Blue for the shadows under the flower petals. Make a light line down the center of the leaf for the main vein. Be sure to soften all the outside edges of the leaves.

Rock -- With pure white put highlights on the rock. Blend some of the edgs in. Since it's a hard rock leave some of the paint unblended to show a hard edge.

Petals -- Detail the petals using a main mixture of White, Brilliant Yellow and a touch of Marigold Yellow. Use more White in the mixture at the end of the petals. In the shaded areas use a little Burnt Sienna. Blend each petal as you go along. This will take some time. Don't forget to use a mixture of White and Brilliant Yellow to put in the centers of the blossoms.

Chipmunk -- Paint the parts of the chipmunk that will be the lightest color with a dark gray made by mixing White with Burnt Umber and Ultramarine Blue.

Eastern Chipmunk

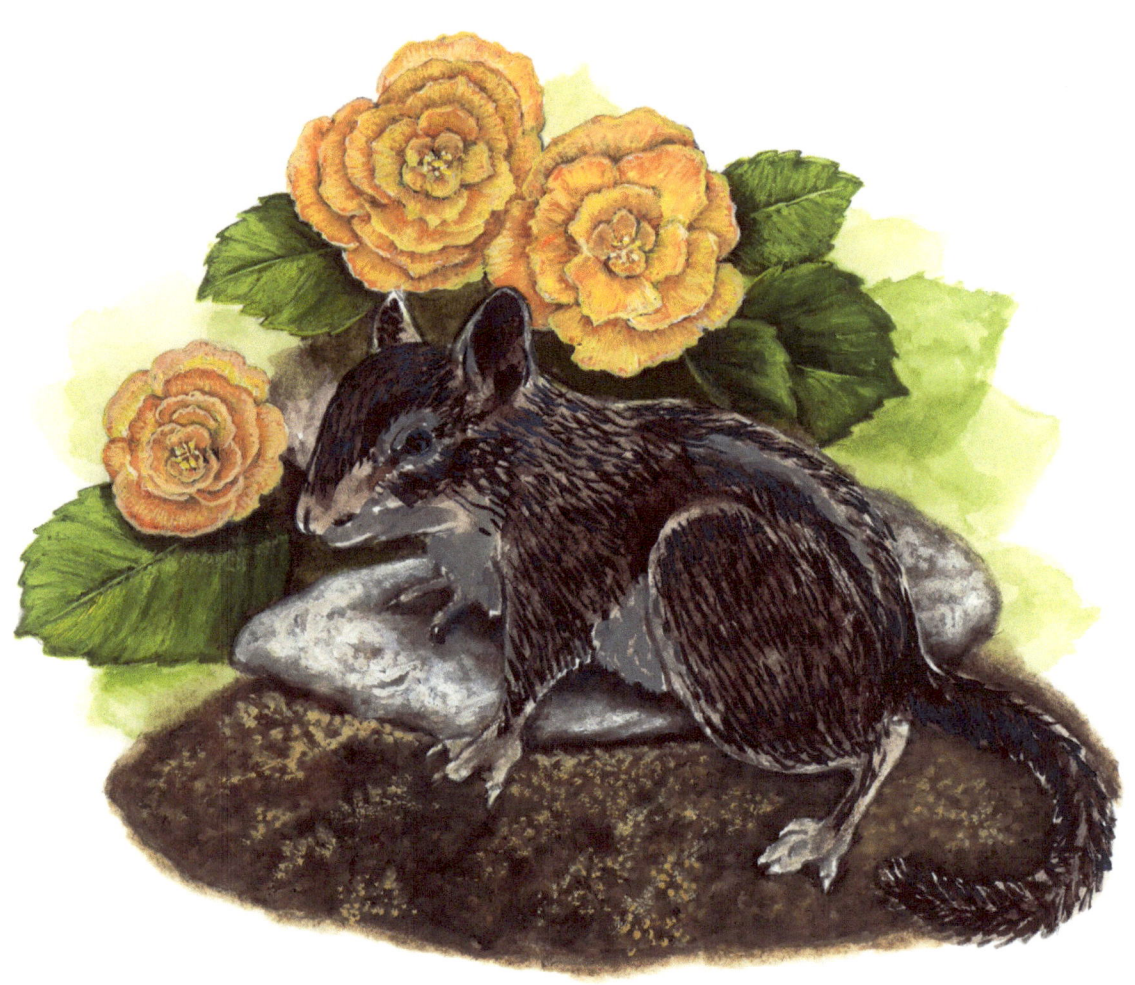

(6)

Chipmunk -- With your darkest value of Burnt Umber and Ultramarine Blue, paint tiny strokes going in the direction of the hair pattern over the entire chipmunk. Darken the inside of the ear.

Eastern Chipmunk

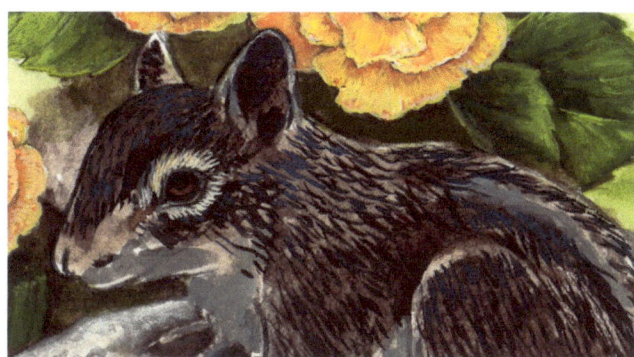

(7)

Eye -- Shape the eye with your darkest value of Burnt Umber and Ultramarine Blue. Add white to the mixture to make gray and paint lines above and below the eye on the rim. With Burnt Sienna paint a semicircle in the lower half of the eye.
With White barely tinted with Yellow Ochre, paint short strokes for the hair radiating out from the eye, both above and below.

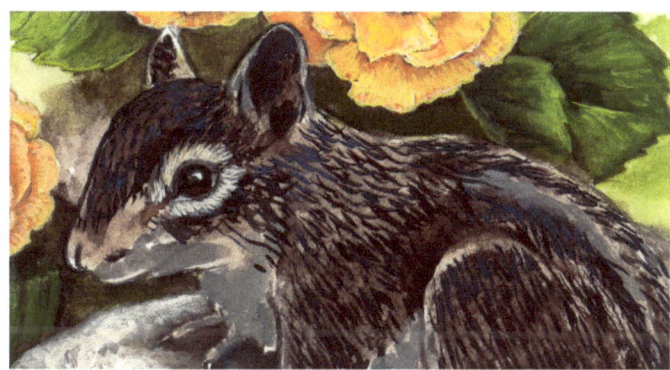

(8)

Gently blend the edges of the Burnt Sienna semicircle in the eye. You want it to barely be noticeable. With pure White paint the highlight in the eye and also highlight the sides of the lower rim around the eye. With a very slightly damp brush, very gently blend the edges of the highlight in the eye. You'll probably need to add a little more White to keep some sparkle. Also, gently blend the white hairs above and below the eye. Don't completely wash away your strokes.

Eastern Chipmunk

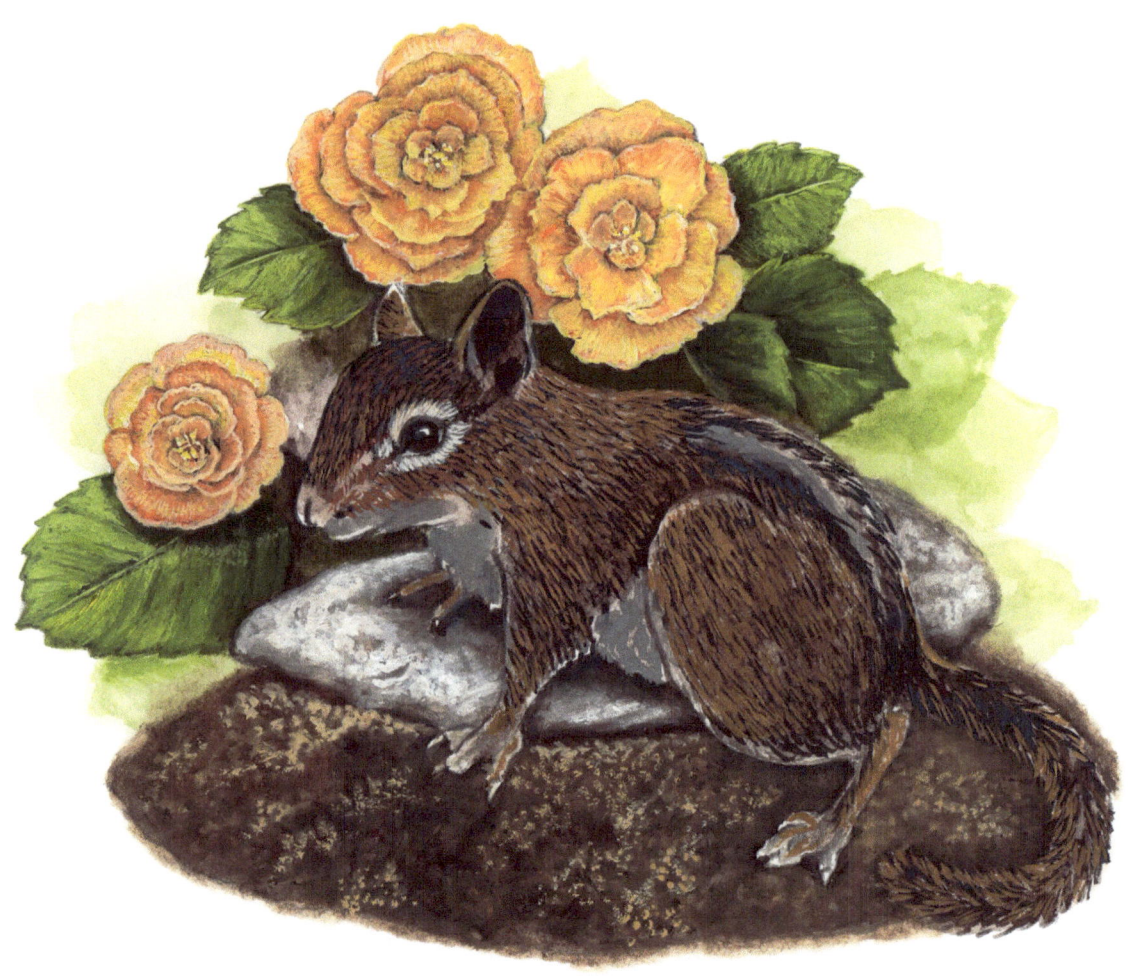

(9)

The Head, Body & Tail -- With thick Yellow Ochre, paint tiny strokes from the nose to the end of the tail going in the direction of the hair pattern. Don't paint over the gray places that will end up being white.

Eastern Chipmunk

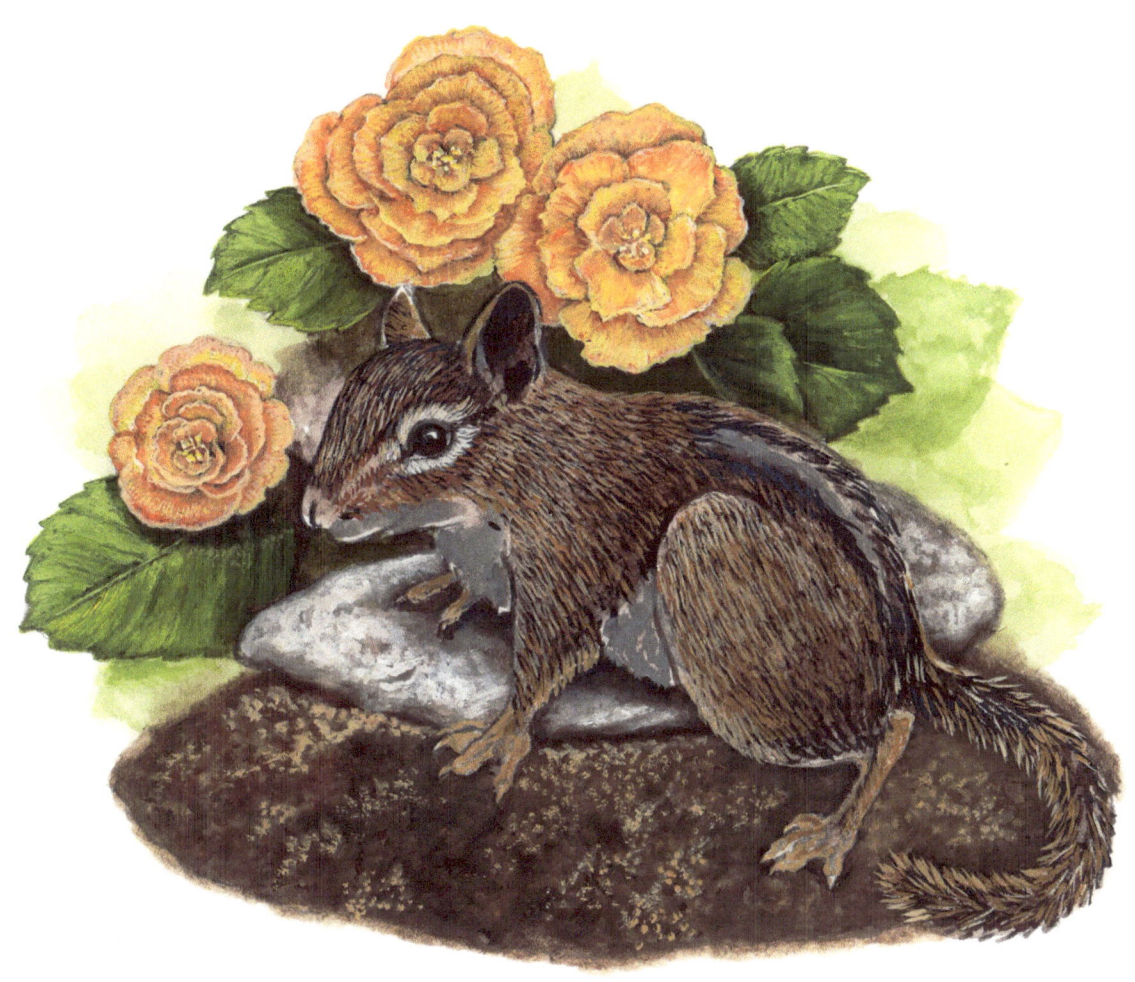

(10)
Blend your strokes a little. With thick White tinted with Yellow Ochre, paint another layer of tiny strokes on the chipmunk, staying away from the areas that will be in shadow.

Eastern Chipmunk

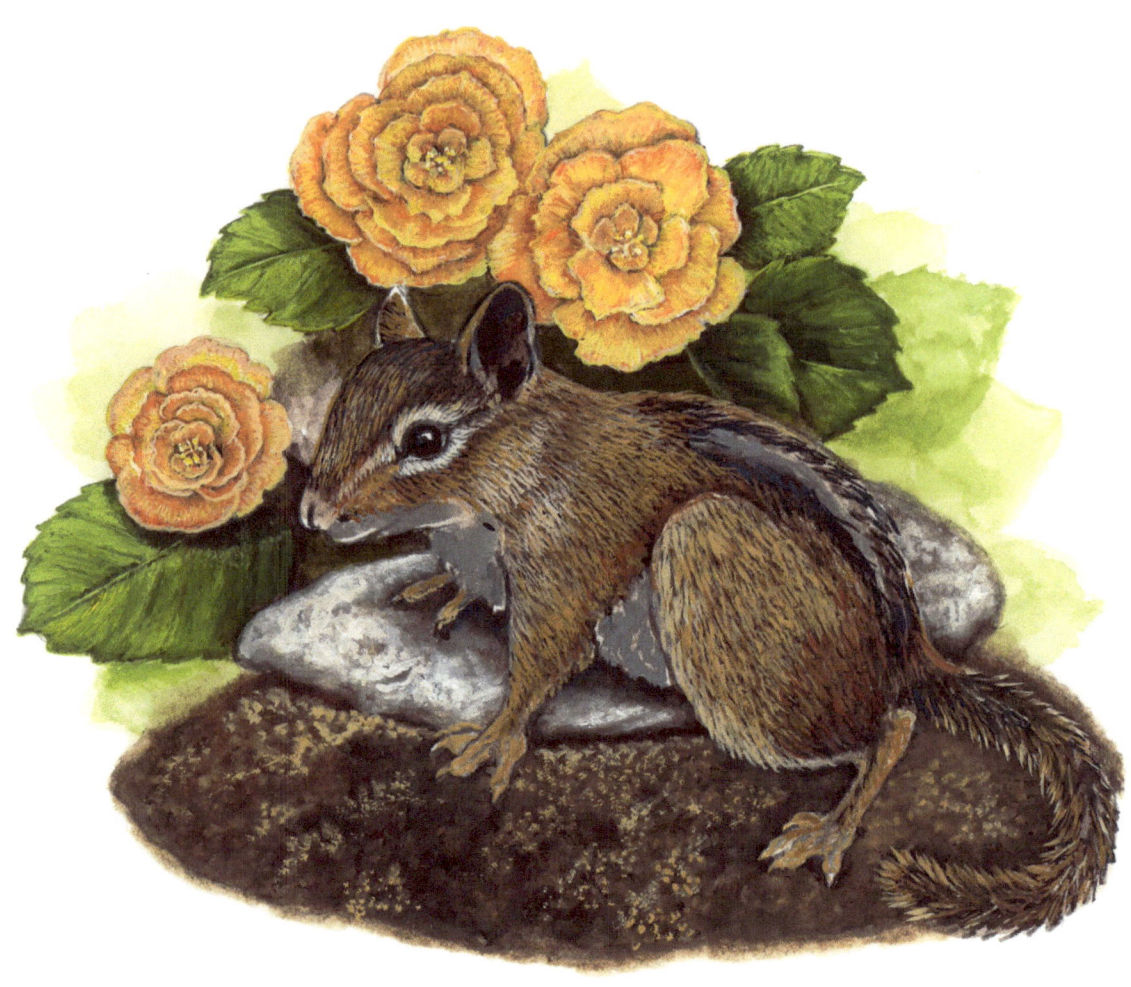

(11)

Gently blend your strokes in a little. Let some of the lower, darker layer show through. This will darken the chipmunk and then it will be ready for the top layer. Use the same White mixed with a little Yellow Ochre mixture to add another layer of light value strokes. Blend them a tiny bit. Use Burnt Sienna to paint shadows in the back of the front leg and on the back of the rump. Blend a little.

Eastern Chipmunk

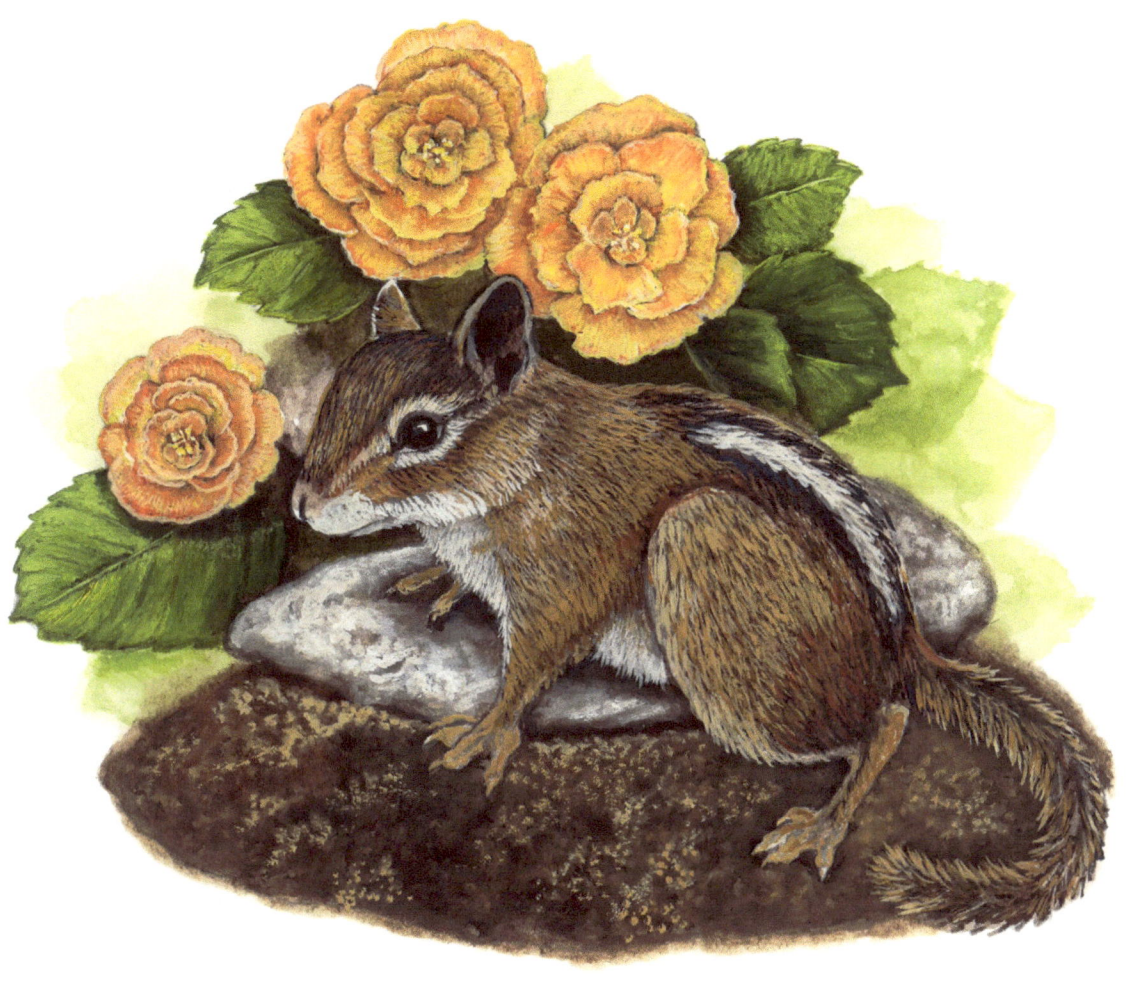

(12)

With pure White, paint short strokes on the muzzle and chin, the underbelly and the stripe on the chipmunk's back. Gently blend your strokes in a little. Blend more under the chin and on the underbelly to make them a little darker.

Eastern Chipmunk

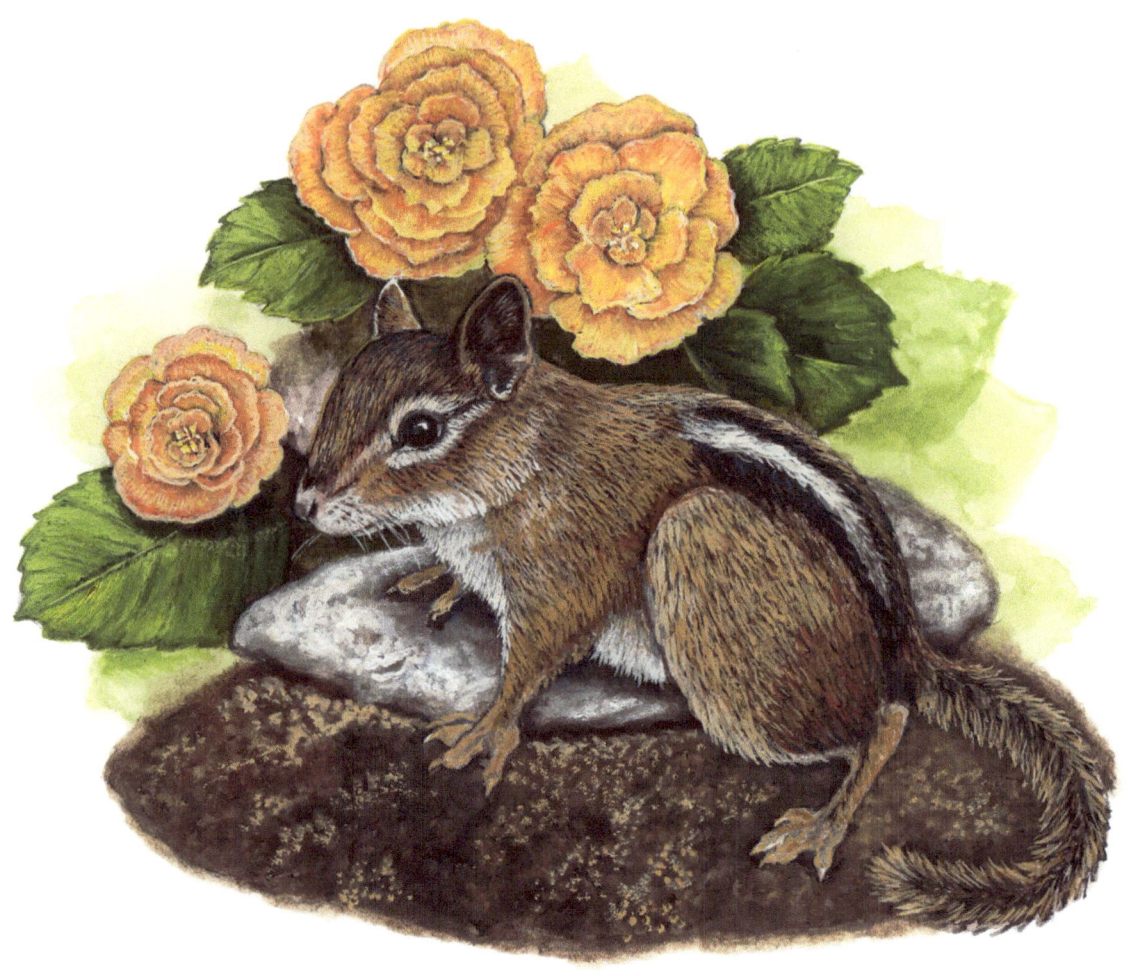

(13)

Finishing the Head -- Using a mixture of Burnt Umber and Ultramarine Blu, paint a dark spot on top of the nose. Blend it in a little. Paint the nostril and put a small touch of gray on the front of the nose. With the tip of your brush, dot on the dark spots at the base of the whiskers. Then use pure White to paint the whisker hairs. I usually get paint on my smallest brush and wipe some of the paint off before I paint the lines.

The Ears in Front -- Use White tinted with Yellow Ochre to paint all around the rim of the ear. Soften the strokes. Use tiny strokes to paint the hairs inside the ear and blend.

Stripes on the back -- Use strokes of Burnt Umber and Ultramarine Blue to make the dark stripes on the back, and use pure White to make the center stripe. Blend your strokes to take the hard edge off. Shade the right side of the white stripe with a little gray and blend again. Paint a dark stripe down the center of the tail.

Eastern Chipmunk

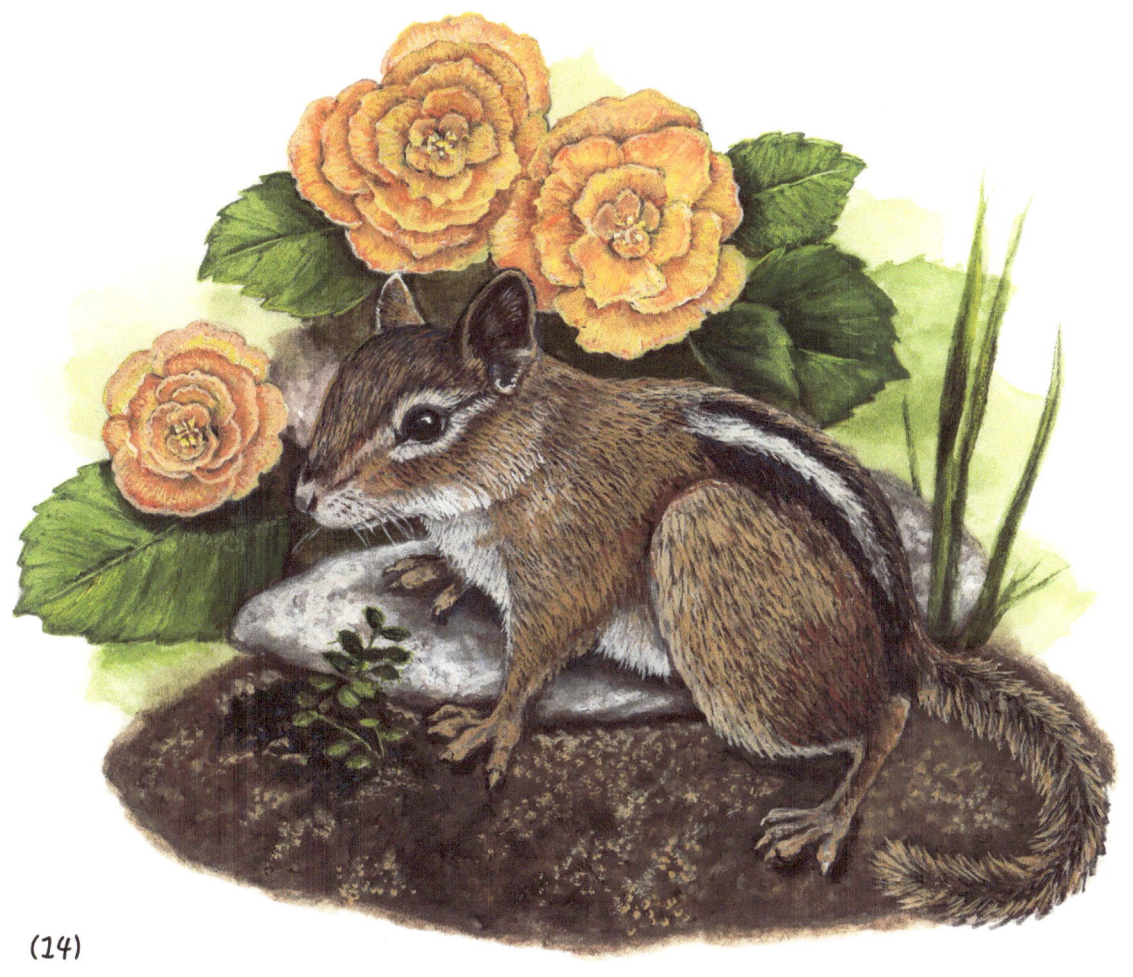

(14)

Paws -- Make sure there's a dark shadow under each toe. Blend the edges of the shadows. Use Yellow Ochre to shape each toe in the paws, using White to make the highlits, Burnt Umber for the shadows. Be sure to blend the hard edges away between your color values.

You could be done at this point but I went ahead and added a few spots of green for more visual interest - the little plant with its tiny leaves in front of the chipmunk's paws and a few blades of grass on the right side.

Always let your painting sit for a while and then go back to it later with a fresh perspective and see what adjustments you need to make.

Cottontail Rabbits

Sylvilagus floridanus

Colors Used: Permanent White, Burnt Umber, Ultramarine Blue,
Olive Green, Brilliant Yellow, Brilliant Violet, Yellow Ochre, Opera Rose

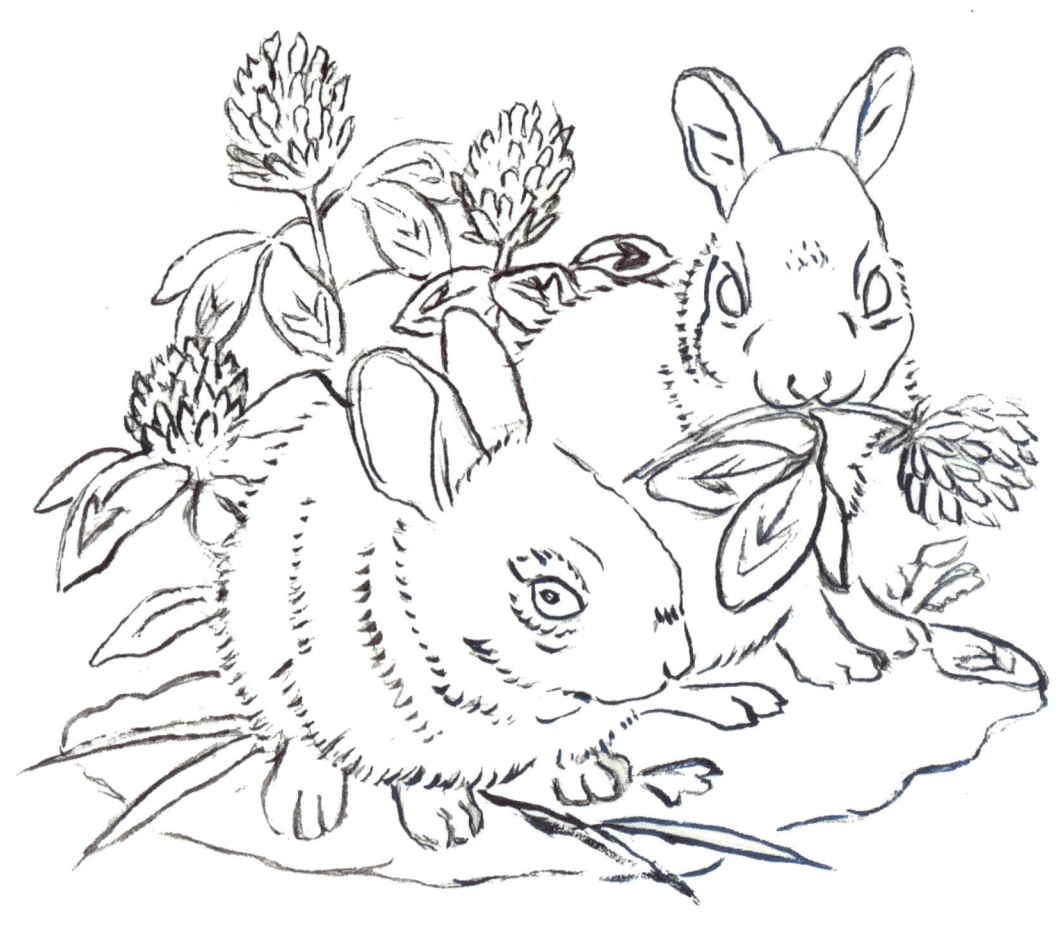

Use this sheet to transfer the image to your sheet of hot press
watercolor paper or illustration board.

Eastern Cottontail Rabbits

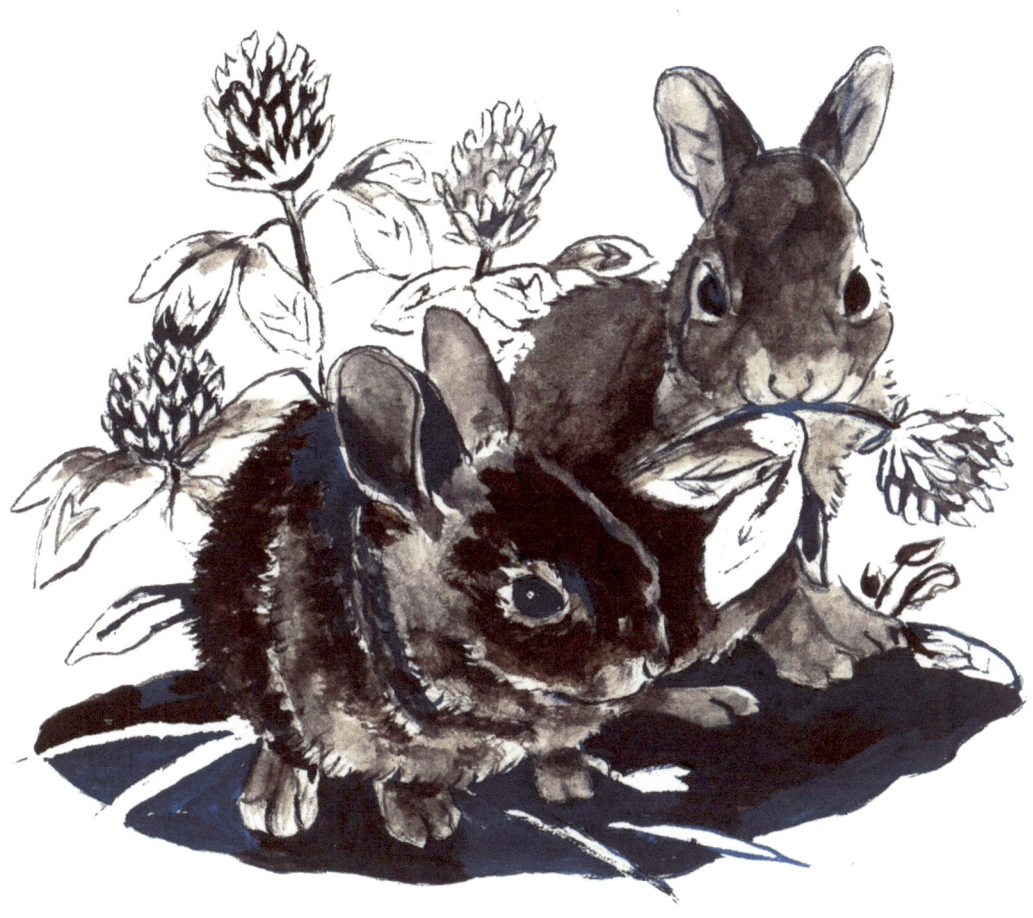

(1)

   The Underpainting --After you've transferred your drawing to your
watercolor paper or board, go over the lines with a dark paint so they
don't get lost when you start layering on the gouache. You can always
skip this step if your pencil lines are dark enough. Then start painting
the underpainting. Use a dark value of a thin mixture of Burnt Umber
and Ultramarine Blue to paint the bottom layer. The painting will look
way too dark -- just remember that this is only the underpainting. Don't
worry about making an even tone. This layer will be painted over.

Eastern Cottontail Rabbits

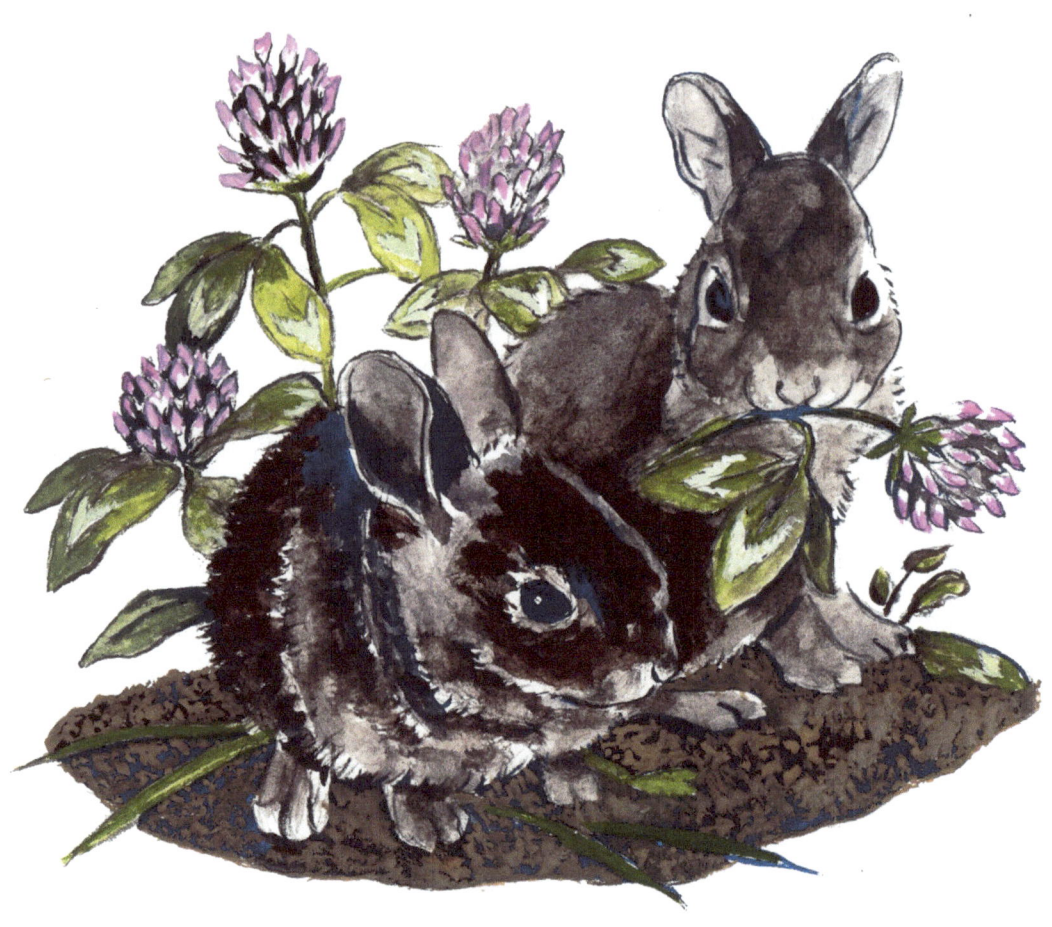

(2)

The Dirt -- With a mixture of Yellow Ochre, White and a little Burnt Umber, paint dots over the lower dark underpainting in the dirt area.

Leaves & Stems -- With a mixture of Olive Green and Brilliant Yellow, roughly paint in the green areas of the leaves and stems. Paint the arrow shaped pattern on the leaves with White tinted with Olive Green.

Clover flower heads -- Use Opera Rose mixed with White to paint the tips of the clover flowers.

At this stage everything is very rough. This is normal.

34

Eastern Cottontail Rabbits

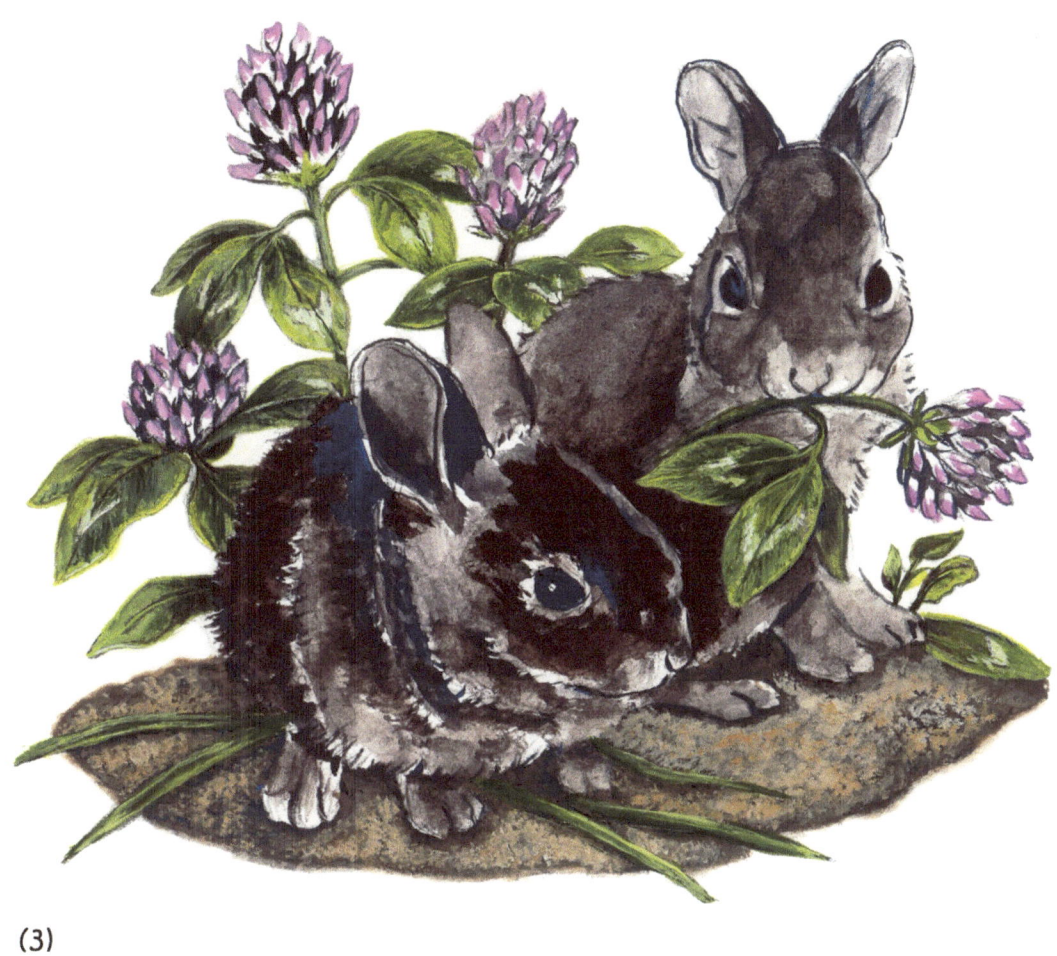

(3)

 The Dirt -- With a thick mixture of White and Yellow Ochre, dry brush on a light value of gouache as the top layer on the dirt. With a slightly damp brush gently blend the three layers. If you lose too much of your lighter or darker values just add more and reblend.

Leaves & Stems -- Use a mixture of White, Olive Green and Brilliant Yellow to make a light green and paint the ends of the leaves and the right side of the stems. Gently blend to smooth your strokes and make subtle transitions. You may have to add more of the dark value in the shadows and reblend and add more of your lightest value toward the tips and reblend until you get the effect you want. Use a light green to make a line along the front edge of the leaves to give them a 3D effect. Also, paint the blades of grass that the young rabbits are sitting on.

Eastern Cottontail Rabbits

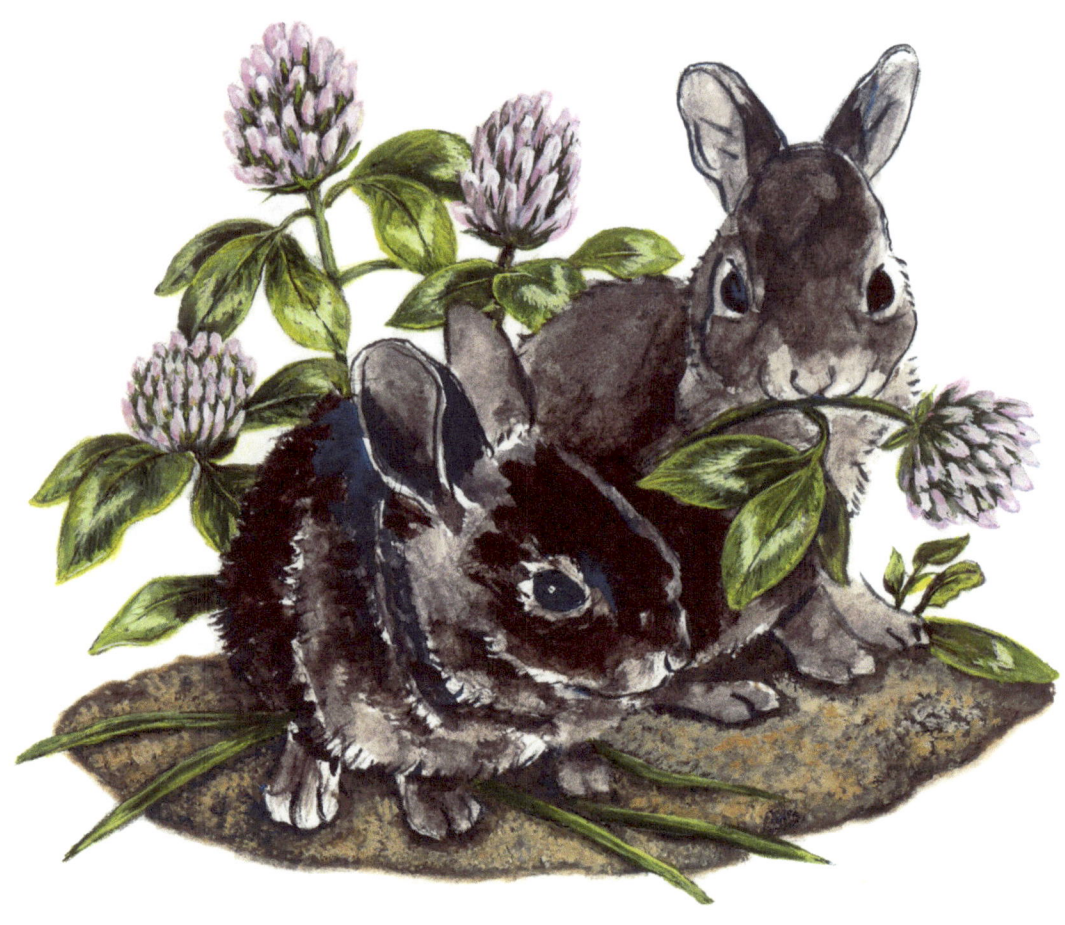

(4)

 To finish the leaves -- With White barely tinted with Olive Green and
Brilliant Yellow, paint the light "arrows" on the clover leaves. Make
your strokes go from the center angled out toward the edges.
Blend the areas in to the rest of the leaf.

Flower heads -- Use White tinted with Opera Rose to finish the
sections of the flowers. Shade them toward the center of the flower
and use almost pure white toward the tips. Blend to soften the edges.
Add Olive Green at the base of each section of the flower and
make a little pointed leaf.

Eastern Cottontail Rabbits

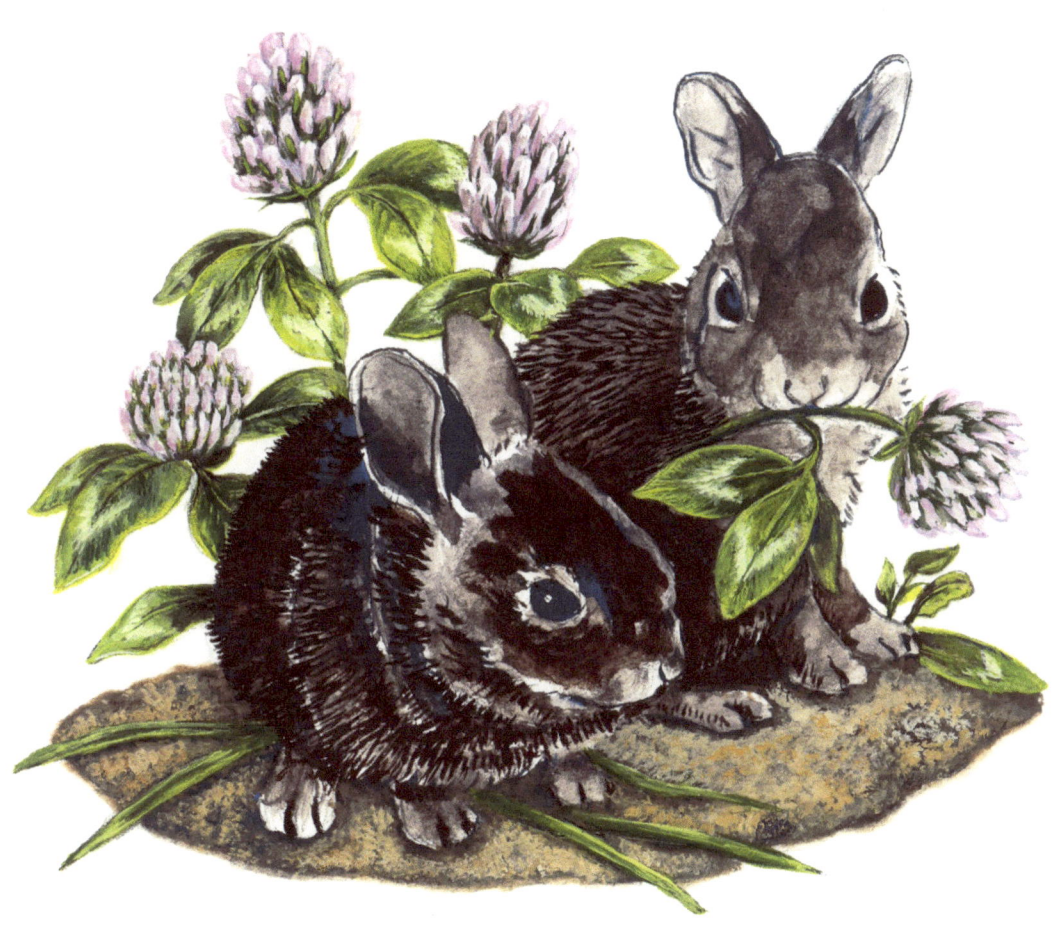

(5)

 Bodies of baby rabbits -- With your darkest value of Burnt Umber
mixed with Ultramarine Blue, paint hairs on the rabbits, always
stroking in the direction of the hair pattern.

Eastern Cottontail Rabbits

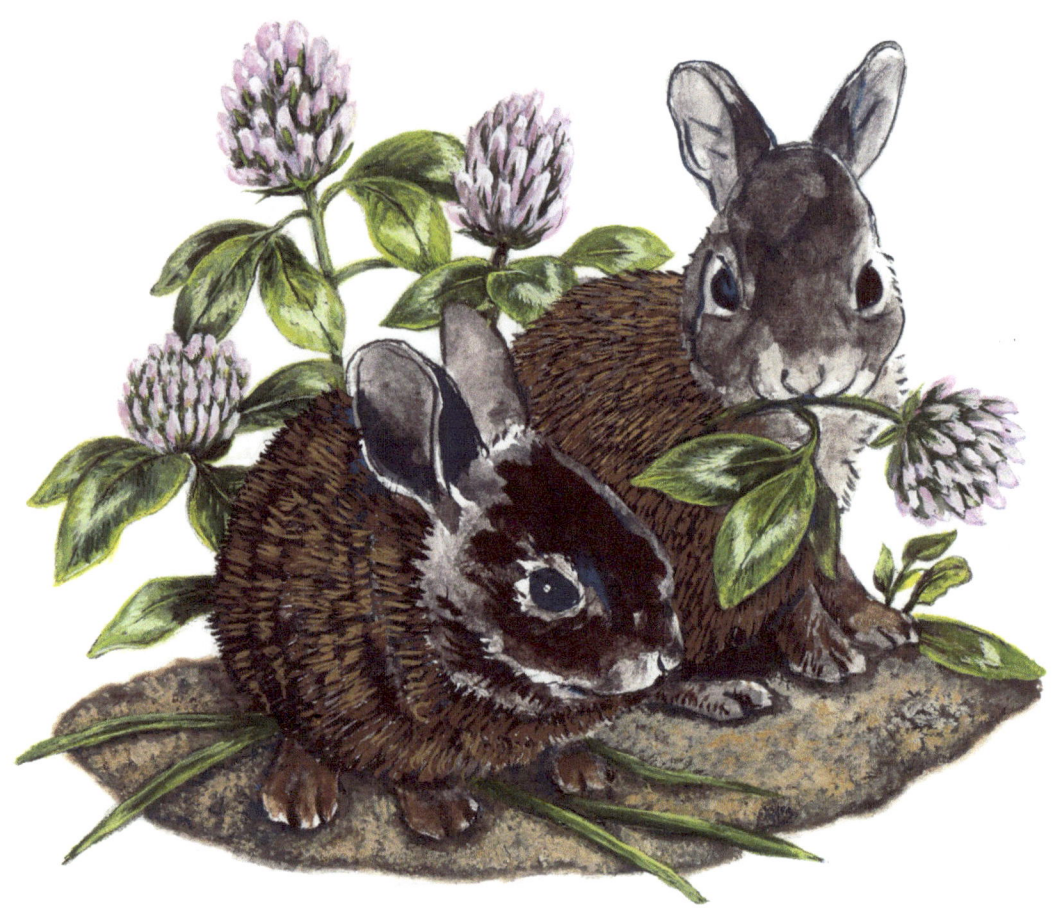

(6)

 Use Yellow Ochre mixed with a touch of Burnt Umber for the next layer. Paint short strokes of this medium value mixture over the bodies of the rabbits, always stroking in the direction of the coat pattern.

Eastern Cottontail Rabbits

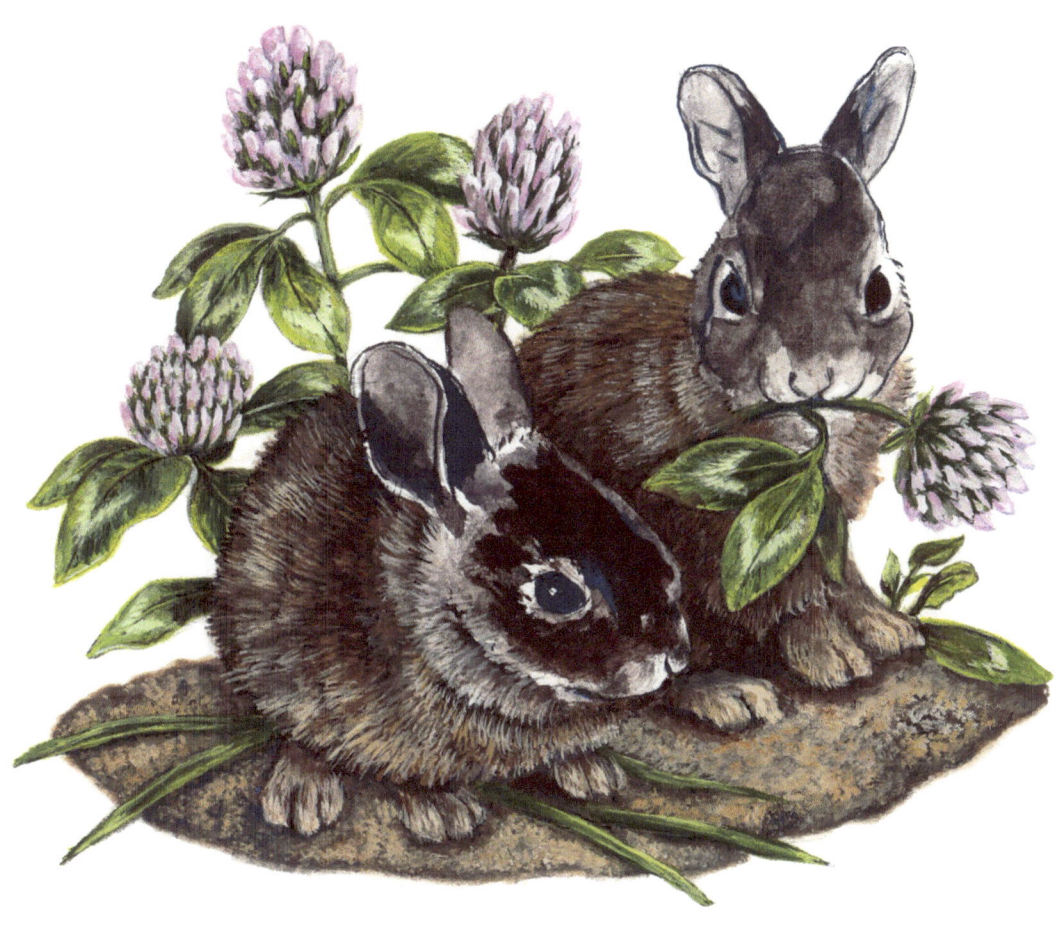

(7)

  Blend your lighter strokes into the darker layer. Then, with White
tinted with Yellow Ochre, paint tiny short strokes over the light
portion of the baby rabbits' bodies and feet. Gently blend them in
using a slightyly damp brush. You may have to restate some of your
dark strokes and blend again.

Eastern Cottontail Rabbits

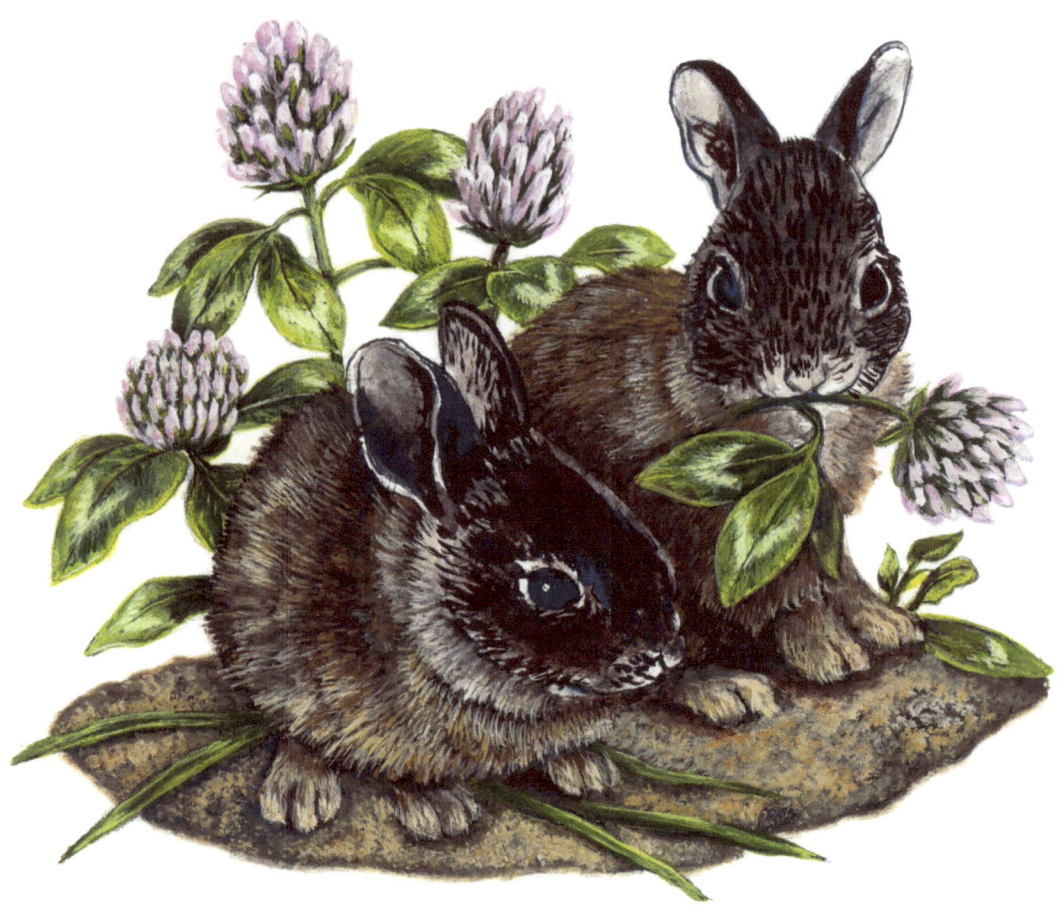

(8)

Heads -- Using a dark value made by mixing Burnt Umber and Ultramarine Blue, make tiny, short strokes on the heads of the rabbits, going in the direction of the coat pattern. Also, paint shadows inside the ears.

Eastern Cottontail Rabbits

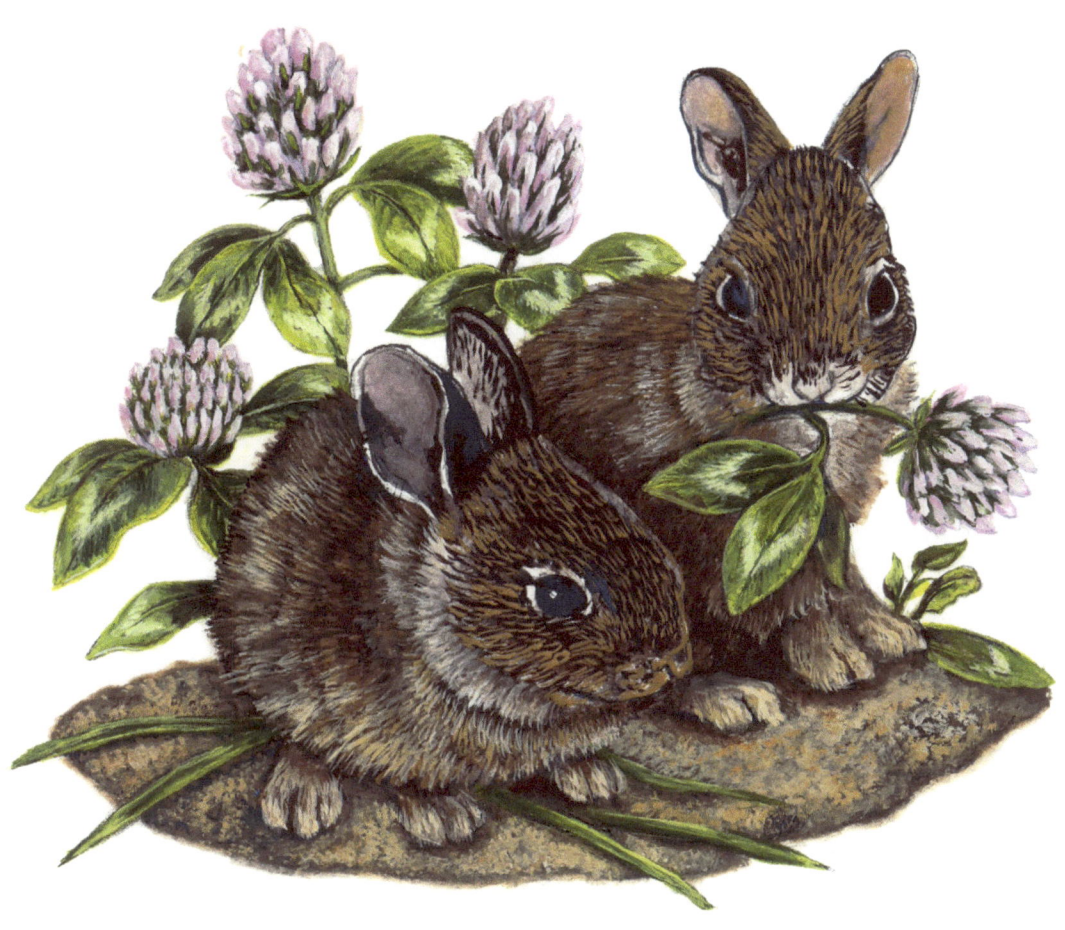

(9)

With thick Yellow Ochre barely tinted with Burnt Umber,
paint the next layer of hairs, always going in the direction
of the coat pattern. Let some of the darker layer show
through. With Opera Rose mixed with a little Yellow Ochre,
paint the inside of the ears.

Eastern Cottontail Rabbits

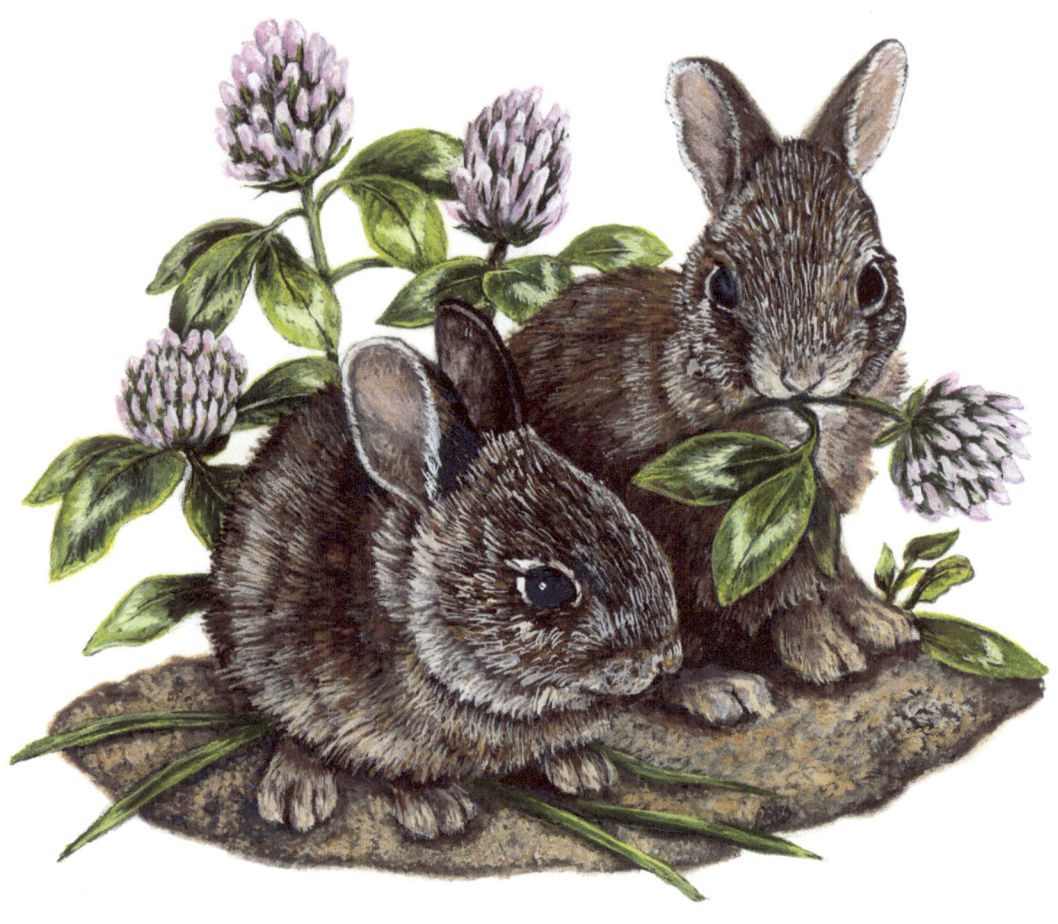

(10)

Head -- With a slightly damp brush, gently blend the hard edges from your strokes. Be careful not to blend too much and lose the dark values underneath. If you do, just repaint them, repaint the Yellow Ochre mixture over them and then reblend. With White barely tinted with Yellow Ochre, paint on the top layer of hairs. Remember -- short, thin strokes of thick paint in the direction of the coat pattern.

Ears -- Use a very light value of White, Opera Rose and Yellow Ochre and paint the inside of the ears. Make your strokes going from the inner side of the ear outward to the edges. Use White to paint tiny strokes along the rim of the ears. Blend them in a little.

42

Eastern Cottontail Rabbits

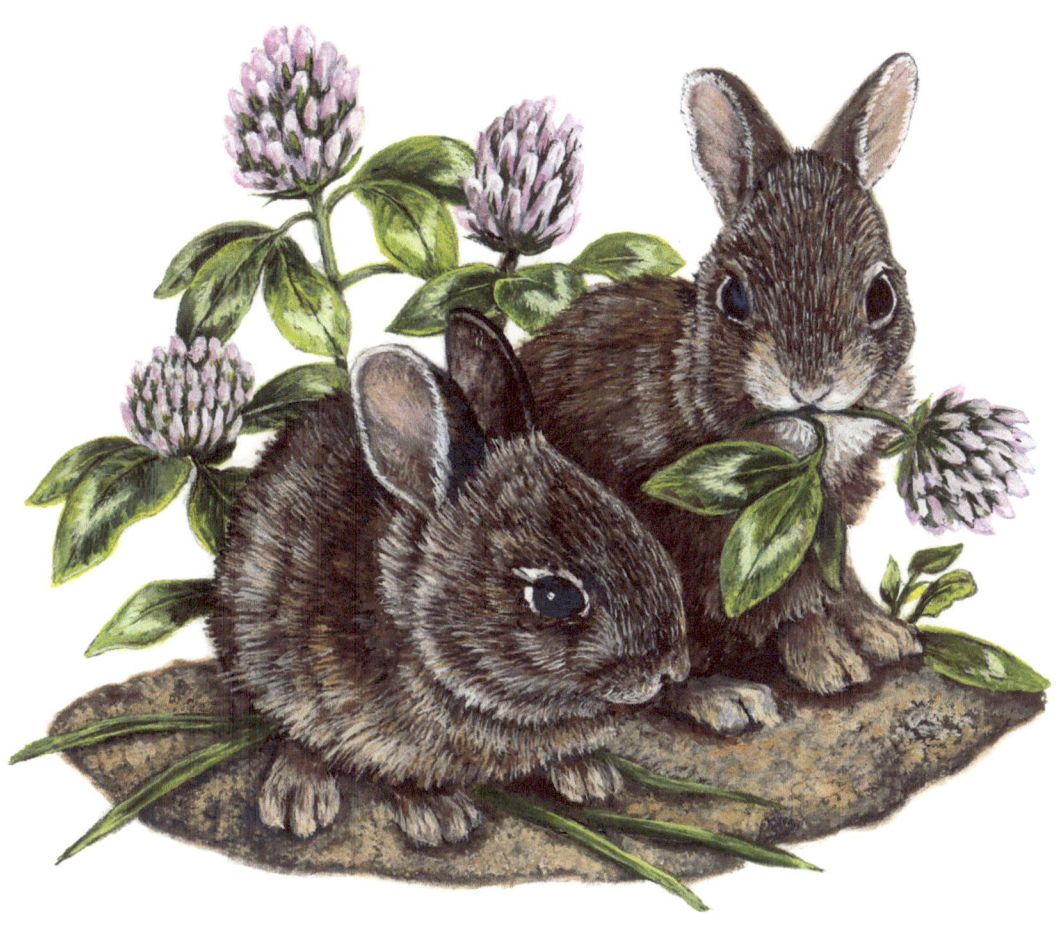

(11)

With a slightly damp brush, blend in the edges of your light value strokes. You'll probably blend some a little too much but that's normal. This is a back and forth process. If you lose too many of your dark lines repaint them. The same goes for your light value strokes. Keep painting the tiny lines and blending until you get the effect you want.

Eastern Cottontail Rabbits

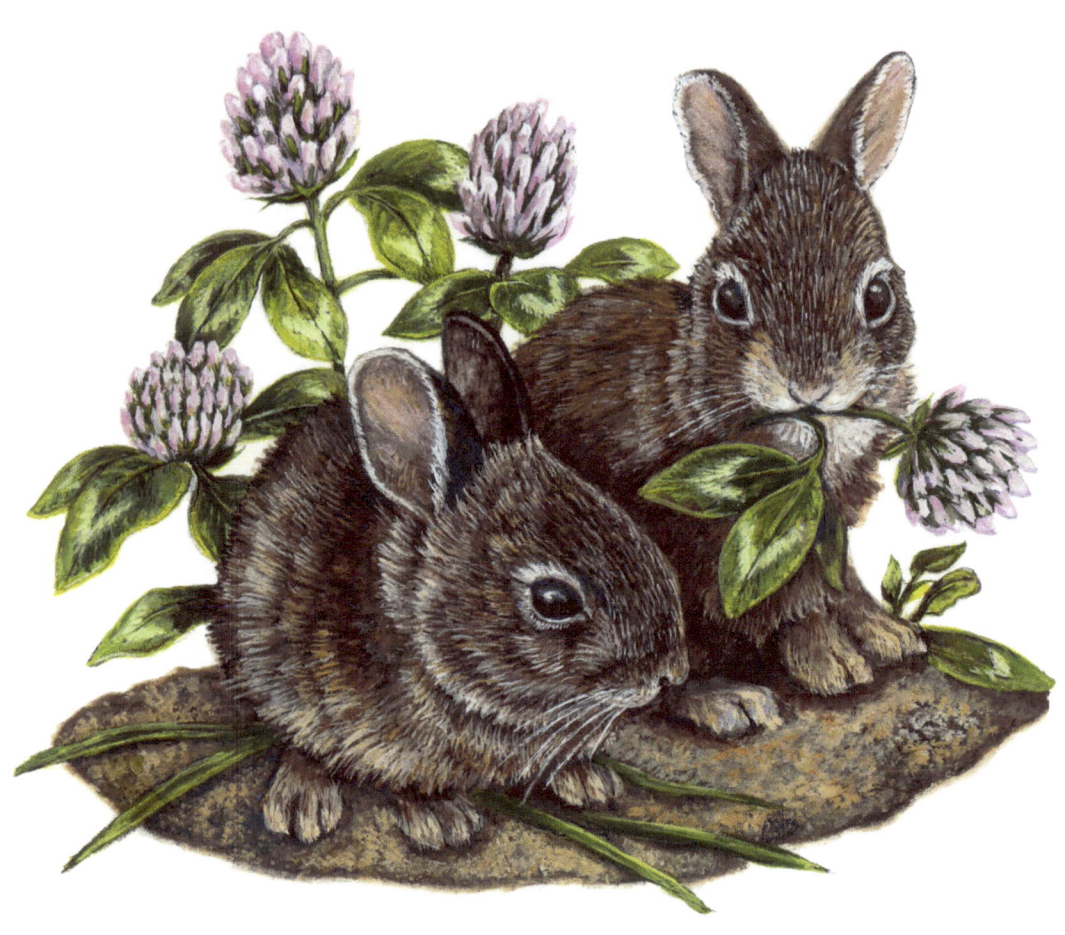

(12)

Eyes & Whiskers - Fine tune the shapes of the eyes using your darkest value of Burnt Umber mixed with Ultramarine Blue. Use Burnt Sienna to make a semicircle that follows the bottom curve of the eye. Very gently blend it in a little until you can barely see it. Use White to put highlights in the eyes, barely softening the edges of the white area to blend a little. With light gray (White mixed with a little Burnt Umber and Ultramarine Blue) paint the lower rims of the eyelids. Wth pure White, paint the hairs above and below the eyes. Always remember to blend off the hard edges of your strokes to make the hairs look more realistic. With your tiniest brush use white to paint in the whiskers, stroking from the muzzle outward.

Wrapping Things Up!

The same techniques you've learned to paint Garden Animals
in Gouache can be used to paint so many of
the creatures and flowers we find around us.
Experiment and find out exactly what works
for you and what subjects most inspire you.

Most of all -- keep painting!

Please check back at
Sound of Wings Studio,
www.soundofwings.com,
for upcoming courses in
painting in gouache.

Thanks!

Sandy

Sandy

Other courses that are currently available are:
    Botanical Illustration in Gouache
    Botanical Illustration in Gouache -- the Four Seasons
    Painting Birds in Gouache
    Painting Animals in Gouache
    Painting Toads and Turtles in Gouache
    Painting Butterflies & Moths in Gouache
    Composing a Natural Science Illustration

And if you have any questions or comments
e mail me at sandy@soundofwings.com
I'd love to hear from you!